R Programming

A Comprehensive Guide to Statistical

Computing

Ryan Campbell

Table of Contents

Introduction to R Programming

In today's data-driven world, the ability to effectively analyze and interpret information is a crucial skill for individuals across various disciplines. R, a powerful and versatile programming language, has emerged as a leading tool for data science and statistical computing. Its extensive capabilities and user-friendly interface make it an ideal platform for both beginners and experienced practitioners.

The Evolution and Significance of R

R's origins can be traced back to the 1970s and the development of the S programming language at Bell Laboratories. Recognizing the limitations of S, Ross Ihaka and Robert Gentleman initiated the R project in the early 1990s, aiming to create a more robust and extensible language. Their efforts culminated in the release of the first official version of R in 1995.

Since its inception, R has undergone continuous development, driven by a vibrant community of contributors. This ongoing evolution has resulted in an extensive collection of packages, specialized libraries that extend R's functionality to address specific domains and tasks. This vast array of packages, coupled with R's core strengths, has propelled it to the forefront of data science and statistical computing.

Navigating the Data Science Landscape

Data science encompasses a broad spectrum of activities, from data collection and wrangling to data modeling and visualization. R's comprehensive capabilities cater to each stage of the data science process, enabling users to effectively handle diverse data types, perform complex analyses, and generate insightful visualizations.

Setting the Stage: Installing and Configuring R Environment

Before embarking on our R programming journey, it is essential to establish a working R environment. This introductory chapter will guide you through the process of installing R and configuring it to suit your needs. We will cover the installation of R on various operating systems, introduce the RStudio interface, and demonstrate basic operations within the R environment.

With a solid foundation established, we will delve into the fundamentals of R programming, exploring data structures, operators, control flow statements, and functions. We will then expand our knowledge by delving into data manipulation techniques, statistical modeling concepts, and graphical visualization methods.

Throughout this journey, we will emphasize hands-on practice, providing ample opportunities to apply newly acquired skills through practical exercises and examples. By the end of this book, you will have gained a comprehensive understanding of R programming and its applications in data science and statistical computing.

Chapter 1: Foundations of R Programming

Welcome to the fascinating world of R programming, where data analysis and statistical computing converge. In this chapter, we will embark on a journey to uncover the fundamental building blocks of R programming, laying a solid foundation for your future explorations in data science.

Unveiling the Power of Variables and Data Types

R programming revolves around variables, which serve as containers for storing data. Just as a box holds various objects, a variable can hold different types of data, such as numbers, characters, or logical values.

Numeric Data: Numeric data encompasses numbers, both whole numbers (integers) and fractional numbers (decimals). For instance, age, height, and temperature are all examples of numeric data.

Code

```
R  age <- 25  Untitled-1  ●
   1      age <- 25
   2      height <- 1.75
   3      temperature <- 22.5
```

Character Data: Character data represents text, including letters, symbols, and punctuation marks. For example, names, addresses, and descriptions are all examples of character data.

Code

```
R  name <- "Alice"  Untitled-1  ●
   1    name <- "Alice"
   2    address <- "123 Main Street"
   3    description <- "A friendly and helpful individual"
```

Logical Data: Logical data represents truth values, either TRUE or FALSE. For instance, whether a person is an adult or a child can be represented using logical data.

Code

```
R  isAdult <- TRUE  Untitled-1  ●
   1    isAdult <- TRUE
   2    isChild <- FALSE
```

Data types play a crucial role in R programming, ensuring that data is handled and interpreted correctly. As we delve deeper into R, we will encounter more complex data types, such as vectors, matrices, and data frames.

Crafting Control: If Statements and Loops in R

Control flow statements dictate the execution order of instructions in a program. R provides two primary control flow statements: if statements and loops.

If Statements: If statements enable conditional execution, allowing us to perform specific actions based on a given condition.

Code

```
if (age >= 18) {
    print("You are an adult")
} else {
    print("You are a child")
}
```

Loops: Loops allow us to repeat a block of code multiple times, often based on a specific condition or a predetermined number of iterations.

Code

```
for (i in 1:10) { Untitled-1
1   for (i in 1:10) {
2     print(i)
3   }
```

Mastering Functions: A Cornerstone of Efficient R Programming

They encapsulate a series of instructions, enabling us to modularize our code, promote code reuse, and enhance code readability.

Code

```
calculateArea <- function(length, width) Untitled-1
1   calculateArea <- function(length, width) {
2     area <- length * width
3     return(area)
4   }
```

To call a function, we simply use its name followed by parentheses enclosing the required arguments.

Code

```
areaOfRectangle <- calculateArea(10, 5)   Untitled-1
1    areaOfRectangle <- calculateArea(10, 5)
2    print(areaOfRectangle)
```

Functions are fundamental building blocks of R programming, allowing us to organize our code effectively and improve the overall structure and maintainability of our programs.

Summary

In this chapter, we have laid the groundwork for R programming by introducing the concepts of variables, data types, control flow statements, and functions. These fundamental elements form the core of R programming and will serve as essential tools throughout our data science journey.

As we progress, we will explore more advanced topics, delve into data manipulation techniques, and uncover the power of data visualization. With each step, we will refine our understanding of R programming and its applications in data analysis and statistical computing.

Chapter 2: Data Mastery with R

Welcome to Chapter 2 of our R programming adventure, where we embark on a journey to conquer the world of data manipulation and transformation. In this chapter, we will delve into the intricacies of data frames and matrices, explore advanced cleaning and preprocessing techniques, and uncover transformative data manipulation strategies.

Decoding Data Frames and Matrices in R

Data frames are the workhorses of R, serving as tabular structures that store and organize data. They consist of rows, representing observations, and columns, representing variables. Data frames provide a convenient way to handle structured data, enabling efficient data manipulation and analysis.

Code

```
# Creating a simple data frame Untitled-1
1    # Creating a simple data frame
2    data <- data.frame(name = c("Alice", "Bob", "Charlie"),
3                         age = c(25, 32, 18),
4                         city = c("New York", "Chicago", "San Francisco"))
```

Matrices are specialized data structures that store rectangular arrays of numerical data. They are particularly useful for mathematical operations and statistical analyses.

Code

```
R  # Creating a matrix  Untitled-1  ●
1    # Creating a matrix
2    matrix <- matrix(c(1, 2, 3, 4, 5, 6), nrow = 2, ncol = 3)
```

Sculpting Data: Advanced Cleaning and Preprocessing Techniques

Data cleaning and preprocessing are essential steps in data preparation, ensuring data quality and consistency before embarking on analysis. R provides a comprehensive set of tools for handling missing values, identifying outliers, and transforming data.

Handling Missing Values: Missing values can distort analyses and lead to erroneous conclusions. R offers various approaches to dealing with missing values, such as imputation, deletion, or using specialized functions.

Code

```
R  # Imputing missing values with the mean  Untitled-1  ●
1      # Imputing missing values with the mean
2      imputedData <- na.replace(data$age, mean(data$age))
```

Identifying Outliers

R provides functions for detecting and removing outliers, ensuring data integrity and preventing undue influence on analyses.

Code

```
R  # Identifying outliers using boxplots  Untitled-1  ●
1      # Identifying outliers using boxplots
2      boxplot(data$age)
```

Data Transformation: Data transformation involves modifying data to improve its suitability for analysis. R offers various techniques, such as scaling, normalization, and log transformation, to enhance data interpretability and consistency.

Code

```
® # Scaling data to a standard normal dist  Untitled-1  ●
   1      # Scaling data to a standard normal distribution
   2      scaledData <- scale(data$age)
```

Beyond Basics: Transformative Data Manipulation Strategies

As we progress beyond the basics, we encounter more sophisticated data manipulation techniques that enable us to reshape and restructure data for specific analyses.

Reshaping Data: Reshaping involves transforming data between different formats, such as converting long to wide format or vice versa. This facilitates comparisons and analysis across different categories.

Code

```
® # Converting long to wide format using r  Untitled-1  ●
   1      # Converting long to wide format using reshape
   2      library(reshape)
   3      wideData <- reshape(data, direction = "wide", timevar = "city", varying = c("age"))
```

Data Joining: Data joining combines data from multiple sources based on common variables. This enables us to integrate information from different datasets and gain a comprehensive understanding.

Code

```
# Merging data frames based on the "name  Untitled-1  ●
1    # Merging data frames based on the "name" column
2    mergedData <- merge(data1, data2, by = "name")
```

Data Subsetting:

Data subsetting extracts specific portions of a dataset based on criteria or conditions. This allows us to focus on relevant subsets of data for targeted analyses.

Code

```
# Selecting rows where "age" is greater  Untitled-1  ●
1    # Selecting rows where "age" is greater than 25
2    subsetData <- data[data$age > 25, ]
```

Data Wrangling: The Art of Data Cleanup

Data wrangling refers to the process of cleaning, transforming, and shaping data to make it more suitable for analysis. It is an essential step in the data science process, as

13

it ensures that the data is accurate, consistent, and appropriately formatted for the task at hand.

Common Data Wrangling Tasks:

- Handling Missing Values: Missing values can arise from various reasons, such as data collection errors or incomplete responses. R provides several methods for dealing with missing values, such as imputation, deletion, or using specialized functions.

- Identifying and Removing Outliers: Outliers are extreme values that deviate significantly from the rest of the data. They can distort analyses and lead to erroneous conclusions. R offers various techniques for detecting and removing outliers, ensuring data integrity and preventing undue influence on analyses.

- Data Transformation: Data transformation involves modifying data to improve its suitability for analysis. Common transformation techniques include scaling, normalization, and log transformation. These techniques can enhance data interpretability and consistency.

Data Reshaping and Joining:

- Reshaping Data: Reshaping involves transforming data between different formats, such as converting long to wide format or vice versa. This facilitates comparisons and analysis across different categories.
- Data Joining: Data joining combines data from multiple sources based on common variables. This enables us to integrate information from different datasets and gain a comprehensive understanding.

Data Subsetting and Aggregation:

- Data Subsetting: Data subsetting extracts specific portions of a dataset based on criteria or conditions. This allows us to focus on relevant subsets of data for targeted analyses.
- Data Aggregation: Data aggregation involves summarizing data by calculating group statistics, such as means, medians, or sums. This enables us to condense large datasets into more manageable summaries and identify patterns or trends.

Data Manipulation Packages:

R offers a wealth of packages specifically designed for data manipulation tasks. Some popular packages include:

- dplyr: A powerful and versatile package for data manipulation, offering a wide range of functions for filtering, selecting, transforming, and summarizing data.
- data.table: A high-performance package for data manipulation, known for its speed and efficiency in handling large datasets.
- reshape2: A package specialized in data reshaping, providing functions for converting between long and wide data formats and performing more complex data transformations.

Data Exploration and Visualization:

Data exploration and visualization are crucial steps in data analysis, allowing us to understand the data's structure, identify patterns, and uncover insights. R provides a rich set of tools for data visualization, including:

- ggplot2: A comprehensive and versatile package for creating sophisticated and aesthetically pleasing visualizations.
- lattice: A flexible and customizable package for creating a wide range of statistical graphics, including scatter plots, boxplots, and time series plots.

- plotly: A package for creating interactive visualizations that can be explored in a web browser.

Data manipulation is a fundamental skill in data science, enabling us to prepare and transform data for effective analysis. By mastering data wrangling techniques, data reshaping and joining strategies, and data subsetting and aggregation methods, we can extract meaningful insights from complex datasets and unlock the power of data-driven decision-making.

Summary

In this chapter, we have expanded our data manipulation skills, mastering advanced data cleaning and preprocessing techniques, and exploring transformative data manipulation strategies. These tools will empower us to effectively prepare and handle data for various data science applications.

As we continue our R programming journey, we will delve into statistical modeling, data visualization, and exploratory data analysis, gaining a comprehensive understanding of the data science process and its applications across diverse domains.

Chapter 3: Visualizing Insights: R's Art of Data Presentation

Welcome to the world of data visualization, where numbers come to life and insights emerge from patterns. In this chapter, we will embark on a journey to master the art of data presentation using R, the powerful language of data science.

Painting with Numbers: Introduction to R Plotting

Data visualization is the art of translating data into visual representations, enabling us to understand complex information and uncover hidden patterns. R provides a comprehensive set of tools for creating a wide range of visualizations, from simple bar charts to sophisticated infographics.

The Basic Building Blocks of R Plots:

- Data: The foundation of any visualization is the data itself. R can handle various data types, including numeric, categorical, and textual data.

- Aesthetics: Aesthetics control the visual appearance of a plot, including colors, shapes, sizes, and line styles. R offers a rich set of aesthetic options to customize plots.

- Geoms: Geoms are the graphical elements that make up a plot, such as points, lines, bars, and annotations. R provides a variety of geoms to represent different types of data and relationships.

Creating a Simple Bar Chart:

Bar charts are a versatile and effective way to compare categorical data. To create a bar chart in R, we can use the ggplot() function and the geom_bar() geom.

Code

```
1   ggplot(data = mpg, aes(x = class, y = hwy)) +
2     geom_bar(stat = "identity")
```

This code will create a bar chart showing the average highway mileage of different car classes.

Beyond Bar Charts

Advanced Data Visualization Techniques

As we move beyond simple bar charts, we can explore a variety of advanced visualization techniques that reveal complex patterns and relationships in data.

- Scatter Plots: Scatter plots are used to visualize the relationship between two numerical variables. They show how the values of one variable change with respect to the other.

Code

```
1   ggplot(data = diamonds, aes(x = carat, y = price)) +
2     geom_point()
```

- Boxplots: Boxplots summarize the distribution of a numerical variable.

Code

```
1   ggplot(data = iris, aes(x = Species, y = Sepal.Length)) +
2     geom_boxplot()
```

- Time Series Plots: Time series plots visualize data that changes over time. They are used to identify trends, seasonality, and patterns in time-dependent data.

Code

```
1   ggplot(data = temperature, aes(x = date, y = temp)) +
2     geom_line()
```

Infographics in R: Telling Stories with Data

Infographics are complex data visualizations that combine multiple elements, such as charts, graphs, and text, to convey a story or message effectively. R provides tools for creating infographics, enabling us to communicate insights in an engaging and impactful manner.

Creating an Interactive Infographic:

R packages like plotly allow us to create interactive infographics that can be explored in a web browser. These interactive visualizations enhance user engagement and enable deeper exploration of data.

Code

```
1   library(plotly)
2   p <- plot(mpg, x = "class", y = "hwy", type = "bar")
3   plotly(p)
```

This code will create an interactive bar chart that allows users to select specific car classes and view their corresponding highway mileage.

Data visualization is an essential skill for data scientists and anyone who works with data. By mastering the art of data presentation, we can transform numbers into meaningful insights and communicate findings effectively. R provides a powerful toolkit for creating a wide range of visualizations, from simple bar charts to sophisticated infographics. As we continue our data science journey, we will refine our visualization skills and discover the power of storytelling with data.

Choosing the Right Visualization for the Task

Selecting the appropriate visualization technique is crucial for effective data communication. Different types of visualizations are better suited for conveying specific types of information. Here are some considerations when choosing a visualization:

Purpose: What is the primary goal of the visualization? Are you trying to compare categories, show trends, or identify patterns?

Data Type: What is the type of data you are visualizing? Numerical data, categorical data, or time-series data?

- Audience: Who is the target audience for the visualization? Their level of expertise and expectations should be considered.

Enhancing Readability and Accessibility

Readability is essential for ensuring that visualizations are easily understood and interpreted.

- Use clear and concise labels: Label axes, legends, and data points clearly to avoid confusion.

- Choose appropriate colors: Use color effectively to distinguish between categories or highlight important features. Avoid color combinations that are difficult to distinguish or may cause visual strain.

- Apply consistent formatting: Maintain consistent formatting across visualizations to create a cohesive presentation.

Accessibility ensures that visualizations are inclusive and can be understood by individuals with diverse abilities. Here are some considerations for enhancing accessibility:

- Use high-contrast color schemes: Employ color combinations that provide sufficient contrast to allow for easy perception, especially for individuals with visual impairments.

- Provide alternative text descriptions: Include alternative text descriptions for images and charts to make them accessible to screen readers used by individuals with visual impairments.

- Consider colorblindness: Avoid relying solely on color to convey information, as individuals with color blindness may not be able to distinguish between certain colors.

Leveraging Interactive Visualizations for Deeper Exploration

Interactive visualizations allow users to explore data in a more dynamic and engaging manner. They enable users to filter, select, and manipulate data points, providing a deeper understanding of patterns and relationships.

- Interactive scatter plots: Users can select specific data points to view their corresponding information or filter the data based on specific criteria.

- Interactive time series plots: Users can zoom in or out of specific time periods, identify trends, and compare values across different time frames.

- Interactive maps: Users can zoom in or out of different geographic regions, hover over data points to view specific information, and filter data based on various criteria.

Conclusion

Data visualization plays a pivotal role in data science, transforming raw data into meaningful representations that facilitate understanding, communication, and decision-making. R offers a comprehensive set of tools for creating a wide range of visualizations, from simple bar charts to sophisticated infographics. By mastering the art of data visualization and applying the principles discussed in this chapter, we can effectively communicate insights, enhance data exploration, and tell compelling data stories.

Chapter 4: Tackling Titans: R in Large Dataset Analysis

Welcome to the realm of big data, where massive datasets hold the key to unlocking groundbreaking insights. In this chapter, we embark on a journey to conquer the challenges of large dataset analysis using R, the versatile language of data science.

Step 1: Recognizing the Signs of Big Data

Before delving into the techniques for handling large datasets, it is crucial to recognize when you are dealing with big data. Here are some telltale signs:

- Data Volume: The sheer size of the dataset, often exceeding gigabytes or even terabytes, makes traditional data analysis methods inefficient.

- Data Complexity: The dataset may contain a variety of data types, complex structures, and intertwined relationships, posing challenges for data management and analysis.

- Data Velocity: The data may be constantly changing and growing, requiring real-time or near-real-time processing capabilities.

Step 2: Embracing Partitioning and Chunking

Partitioning and chunking are fundamental strategies for handling large datasets. This reduces the memory footprint and allows for parallel processing, significantly improving computational efficiency.

Step 3: Leveraging Efficient Data Storage Formats

The way data is stored can significantly impact processing speed. Parquet, a columnar data storage format, offers efficient data compression and random access capabilities, making it ideal for large datasets.

Step 4: Utilizing Specialized Data Analysis Packages

R offers several packages specifically designed for handling large datasets, such as dplyr, data.table, and bigmemory. These packages provide optimized functions for data manipulation and analysis, enabling efficient processing of large data volumes.

Step 5: Employing Sampling Techniques

When dealing with extremely large datasets, analyzing the entire dataset may be impractical or unnecessary. Sampling techniques, such as random sampling or stratified sampling, allow us to extract representative subsets of data for analysis.

Step 6: Exploring Cloud-Based Solutions

Cloud computing platforms, such as Amazon Web Services (AWS) and Google Cloud Platform (GCP), offer scalable and cost-effective solutions for storing and analyzing large datasets. These platforms provide parallel processing capabilities and access to specialized tools for big data analysis.

Step 7: Optimizing Code and Algorithms

Efficient code writing practices and the selection of appropriate algorithms are crucial for optimizing performance when dealing with large datasets. Data scientists should strive to minimize unnecessary data processing steps, employ vectorized operations, and choose algorithms with low computational complexity.

Step 8: Utilizing Distributed Computing Frameworks

Distributed computing frameworks, such as Apache Spark and Apache Hadoop, are designed for processing large datasets across multiple machines or nodes. These frameworks partition data and distribute computations, significantly reducing processing time and enabling efficient analysis of massive datasets.

Step 9: Embracing Continuous Learning and Adaptation

The field of big data is constantly evolving, with new tools and techniques emerging regularly. Data scientists should stay abreast of these advancements and adapt their skills to effectively handle the ever-growing volume and complexity of data.

Navigating the world of large dataset analysis requires a combination of strategic planning, specialized tools, and efficient coding practices. By adopting the strategies and techniques discussed in this chapter, data scientists can effectively tackle the challenges of big data and extract meaningful insights from massive datasets, shaping the future of data-driven decision-making.

Unleashing the Power of Parallel Computing in R

In the realm of big data analysis, parallel computing has emerged as a game-changer, enabling the efficient processing of massive datasets that would otherwise be intractable for traditional single-threaded approaches. R, the versatile language of data science, offers several avenues for leveraging parallel computing to accelerate data analysis and statistical computations.

Harnessing the Power of Packages

R provides a rich ecosystem of packages that harness the power of parallel computing for various data analysis tasks. These packages, such as parallel, doParallel, and foreach, enable users to distribute computations across multiple cores or even multiple machines, significantly reducing processing time.

Code

```
1  library(parallel)
2
3  # Create a parallel backend with 4 cores
4  cl <- makeCluster(4)
5  # Perform parallel computations on a cluster
6  result <- parSapply(cl, 1:10, function(x) x^2)
7
8  # Stop the parallel cluster
9  stopCluster(cl)
```

This code snippet demonstrates how to perform parallel computations on a cluster of four cores. The parSapply() function distributes the task of squaring each number from 1 to 10 across the available cores, resulting in a significant performance improvement compared to a single-threaded approach.

Parallel Processing with GPUs

Graphics processing units (GPUs) have revolutionized parallel computing, offering exceptional computational power for data-intensive tasks. R integrates with GPU computing frameworks, such as CUDA and OpenCL, enabling users to harness the power of GPUs for accelerating statistical computations.

Code

```
1   library(gpuR)
2   # Load a matrix onto the GPU
3   gpuMatrix <- gpuMatrix(x)
4   # Perform matrix multiplication on the GPU
5   result <- gpuMatrix %*% gpuMatrix
6   # Copy the result back to the CPU
7   result <- as.matrix(result)
```

This code snippet illustrates how to perform matrix multiplication on a GPU using the gpuR package. The gpuMatrix() function transfers the matrix to the GPU memory, and the matrix multiplication operation is performed on the GPU, exploiting its parallel processing capabilities.

Statistical Prowess: Large Dataset Analysis and Beyond

Parallel computing empowers R to tackle complex statistical analyses with large datasets, enabling researchers to explore new frontiers in various fields.

- Genome-Wide Association Studies (GWAS): Parallel computing facilitates the analysis of massive genetic datasets, enabling researchers to identify genetic variants associated with complex diseases.

Machine Learning and Artificial Intelligence (ML/AI)

Parallel processing accelerates the training and evaluation of ML/AI models, allowing researchers to build sophisticated algorithms for predictive analytics and pattern recognition.

- Risk Assessment and Simulations: Parallel computing enables the rapid simulation of complex systems and the evaluation of risk scenarios, aiding in decision-making and policy formulation.

Embracing Parallel Computing for Data-Driven Innovation

Parallel computing has become an indispensable tool for data scientists, enabling them to extract insights from massive datasets and address challenging problems across diverse domains. By embracing parallel computing in R, researchers can accelerate their research endeavors, fuel innovation, and make a significant impact on society.

Chapter 5: Riding the Machine Learning Wave with R

Welcome to the captivating realm of machine learning, where algorithms learn from data to make predictions and uncover hidden patterns. In this chapter, we embark on a journey to explore the world of supervised learning using R, the versatile language of data science.

Supervised Learning

Unveiling the Secrets of Labeled Data

Supervised learning, a cornerstone of machine learning, involves training an algorithm to map inputs to desired outputs using labeled data. The algorithm learns from a set of examples, each with an associated outcome, and then generalizes this knowledge to predict outcomes for new, unseen data.

Exploring the Landscape of Supervised Learning Algorithms

R offers a rich collection of supervised learning algorithms, each tailored for specific tasks and data types. Let's delve into some of the most prominent algorithms:

- Linear Regression: A versatile algorithm for predicting continuous numerical values, such as predicting house prices based on size and features.

- Logistic Regression: A powerful tool for binary classification tasks, such as predicting whether an email is spam or not based on its content.

- Decision Trees: Intuitive algorithms that partition data into segments based on decision rules, making them interpretable and suitable for various classification tasks.

- Random Forests: An ensemble method that combines multiple decision trees, improving predictive accuracy and robustness.

- Support Vector Machines (SVMs): Powerful classifiers that can handle complex nonlinear relationships between data points, making them effective for both classification and regression tasks.

The Supervised Learning Workflow: From Data to Insights

The supervised learning workflow involves a series of steps:

1. Data Preparation: Cleaning, preprocessing, and transforming data to ensure its quality and suitability for analysis.

2. Exploratory Data Analysis (EDA): Understanding the data's characteristics, identifying patterns, and detecting potential issues.

3. Feature Engineering: Creating or transforming features to improve the algorithm's ability to learn from the data.

4. Model Training: Training the chosen algorithm on the prepared data, allowing it to learn the relationships between inputs and outputs.

5. Model Evaluation: Assessing the model's performance on unseen data to evaluate its generalization ability.

6. Model Deployment: Integrating the model into an application or system to make predictions on new data.

R Packages for Supervised Learning: A Treasure Trove of Tools

R provides a comprehensive collection of packages tailored for supervised learning tasks. These packages offer user-friendly functions for data preparation, model training, evaluation, and optimization. Popular packages include:

- caret: A comprehensive package for training, tuning, and evaluating a wide range of machine learning models.

- e1071: A versatile package for various machine learning algorithms, including linear and logistic regression, decision trees, and support vector machines.

- randomForest: A dedicated package for building and analyzing random forest models.

- glmnet: A package for fitting generalized linear models with elastic net regularization, useful for feature selection and model regularization.

Supervised Learning in Action: Real-World Applications

Supervised learning has revolutionized various industries and applications:

- Predictive Analytics: Predicting future trends, customer behavior, and risk factors.

- Spam Filtering: Identifying and filtering unwanted emails based on their content.

- Medical Diagnosis: Assisting medical professionals in diagnosing diseases based on patient data and symptoms.

- Fraud Detection: Identifying fraudulent transactions and activities in financial systems.

- Recommender Systems: Suggesting relevant products, movies, or music based on user preferences.

Supervised learning, empowered by R, has become an indispensable tool for data scientists and practitioners across diverse fields. By harnessing the power of supervised learning algorithms, we can extract knowledge from data, make informed predictions, and uncover hidden patterns that drive innovation and decision-making. As we continue our journey in the realm of machine learning, we will delve into more sophisticated techniques, explore unsupervised learning, and uncover the transformative power of data-driven modeling.

Crafting Predictive Models: From Basics to Advanced Techniques

The art of crafting predictive models involves a combination of data exploration, feature engineering, algorithm selection, and hyperparameter optimization. R provides a comprehensive set of tools to support each stage of this process.

Data Exploration and Feature Engineering: Laying the Foundation

Data exploration is crucial for understanding the characteristics of the data and identifying potential patterns or relationships. R offers a variety of data visualization techniques, such as scatter plots, histograms, and boxplots, to visualize the data and uncover insights.

Feature engineering involves creating or transforming features to improve the predictive power of the model. This may involve scaling features, imputing missing values, or creating new features based on existing ones. R provides several packages, such as dplyr and data.table, for data manipulation and feature engineering tasks.

Algorithm Selection: Choosing the Right Tool for the Job

For instance, linear regression is suitable for predicting continuous numerical values, while logistic regression is appropriate for binary classification tasks. R offers a wide range of supervised learning algorithms, including decision trees, random forests, and support vector machines.

Hyperparameter Optimization: Refining the Model's Performance

Optimizing hyperparameters involves searching for the combination of values that produces the best model performance. R provides various methods for hyperparameter optimization, such as grid search and random search.

Evaluation Mastery: Assessing Model Performance in R

Model evaluation is essential for ensuring that the model generalizes well to unseen data. R offers a variety of metrics for evaluating model performance, depending on the task.

Classification Metrics

Accuracy measures the proportion of correctly classified instances, while precision and recall assess the model's ability to identify positive and negative cases correctly, respectively. The F1-score balances precision and recall.

Regression Metrics

For regression tasks, common metrics include mean squared error (MSE), root mean squared error (RMSE), and mean absolute error (MAE). These metrics measure the difference between the predicted values and the actual values.

Cross-Validation Techniques: Assessing Generalization Ability

Cross-validation is a technique for estimating the generalization ability of a model. It involves splitting the data into multiple folds and training the model on different folds, using the remaining folds for evaluation. This process provides a more reliable estimate of the model's performance on unseen data.

R provides various cross-validation functions, such as kfold() and repeated_cv(), enabling data scientists to assess model performance under different data splits.

Conclusion

Crafting predictive models is an iterative process that involves data exploration, feature engineering, algorithm selection, hyperparameter optimization, and model evaluation. R provides a comprehensive set of tools to support each stage of this process, enabling data scientists to build robust and reliable predictive models that extract meaningful insights from data.

Chapter 6: Advanced Topics in R Programming

Welcome to the realm of advanced R programming, where we explore the frontiers of data science and uncover the transformative power of R to tackle complex problems and shape the future of data-driven decision-making.

Parallel Universe:

Mastering Parallel Computing in R

In the era of big data, parallel computing has emerged as an indispensable tool for data scientists, enabling them to process massive datasets efficiently and extract meaningful insights. R embraces parallel computing through various strategies and packages, empowering data scientists to harness the power of multiple cores, GPUs, and distributed computing frameworks.

Harnessing Multiple Cores

Unleashing the Power of Multicore Processors

Multicore processors, with multiple cores working in parallel, provide significant performance improvements for computationally intensive tasks. R offers packages like parallel and doParallel to distribute computations across multiple cores, enabling faster data analysis and model training.

GPU Computing

Accelerating Data Processing with Graphics Processing Units

Graphics processing units (GPUs), initially designed for graphics rendering, have revolutionized parallel computing due to their massive parallel processing capabilities. R integrates with GPU computing frameworks, such as CUDA and OpenCL, enabling data scientists to leverage the power of GPUs for accelerating statistical computations and machine learning tasks.

Distributed Computing Frameworks: Tackling Massive Datasets Across Machines

Distributed computing frameworks, such as Apache Spark and Apache Hadoop, are designed to process massive datasets across multiple machines or nodes. R integrates with these frameworks, enabling data scientists to distribute computations across a cluster of machines, significantly reducing processing time and enabling efficient analysis of large datasets.

Synergy in Data Science

Integrating R with Other Tools

R's versatility extends beyond its own capabilities, as it seamlessly integrates with various tools and frameworks, fostering a collaborative and powerful data science ecosystem.

RStudio is a popular IDE for R, providing a user-friendly interface, code editing tools, and debugging functionalities, enhancing productivity and code development.

R Packages: Extending R's Capabilities with Specialized Tools

R's rich ecosystem of packages provides a vast array of specialized tools for various data science tasks, ranging from data manipulation and visualization to machine learning and statistical modeling.

Integration with Databases and APIs: Accessing and Processing External Data

R can connect to various databases and APIs, enabling data scientists to access, process, and analyze data stored in external sources, such as SQL databases and cloud-based data storage platforms.

The Future Beckons: Emerging Trends and Innovations in R Programming

R's continuous evolution brings forth exciting trends and innovations that shape the future of data science.

R in Production: Deploying R Models for Real-World Applications

R is increasingly being used to deploy machine learning models into production environments, making predictions and insights accessible to real-world applications.

Cloud-Based R Solutions: Leveraging Scalable Computing Power

Cloud-based R solutions, such as Amazon SageMaker and Google Cloud AI Platform, offer scalable computing resources and pre-built tools for R-based data science, enabling data scientists to focus on analysis and modeling without managing infrastructure.

R for Machine Learning: Advancing Predictive Analytics and AI

R continues to evolve as a powerful platform for machine learning, with new algorithms, techniques, and tools emerging to address increasingly complex problems.

Conclusion

R's journey into the realm of advanced topics has transformed it into a powerful and versatile tool for data scientists, empowering them to tackle complex problems, extract meaningful insights from massive datasets, and shape the future of data-driven decision-making. As we continue to explore the frontiers of data science, R will remain an indispensable tool, adapting and evolving to address the ever-growing challenges and opportunities in the ever-changing world of data.

Chapter 7: Capstone: Bringing It All Together

In this chapter, we take a moment to reflect on the transformative journey you've undertaken in mastering R programming. From the foundational concepts of data structures and functions to the intricate domains of data manipulation and visualization, your proficiency has evolved into a comprehensive skill set. This chapter serves as a retrospective, encouraging you to appreciate the progress made and providing insights into the significance of your newfound expertise.

Reflections on the R Programming Journey

Consider the evolution of your proficiency in R programming. Remember the initial challenges of deciphering syntax and understanding the logic behind the code. Think about the breakthrough moments when seemingly complex concepts started to make sense. The journey has not only equipped you with technical skills but also instilled problem-solving and critical-thinking abilities.

Navigating the vast R ecosystem has likely been an eye-opening experience. From a myriad of packages to diverse applications in statistics, machine learning, and data visualization, R is a powerful tool with boundless possibilities. Reflect on the packages you've explored and those that align with your specific interests and career goals. Understanding the ecosystem goes beyond learning specific functions; it's about grasping the underlying principles that empower you to adapt and innovate.

Case Studies:

Applying R to Real-World Challenges

To solidify your understanding and demonstrate the practical application of R programming, let's delve into real-world case studies. Each case study presents a unique challenge that R can address, showcasing the language's versatility and applicability across various domains.

Predictive Analytics in Finance

Explore the use of R in the financial sector through a case study on predictive analytics. Witness how statistical models and machine learning algorithms can be employed to forecast stock prices, assess risk, and make informed investment decisions. Gain insights into the integration of external data sources and the development of robust models that withstand the complexities of financial markets.

Epidemiological Modeling

Delve into the realm of epidemiology and public health by examining a case study on epidemiological modeling. Learn how R facilitates the creation and analysis of models to predict disease spread, optimize resource allocation, and evaluate intervention strategies. Witness the impact of data visualization in communicating complex information to stakeholders and the general public.

Text Mining for Business Insights

Uncover the power of text mining in deriving business insights. Through a case study, discover how R can be employed to analyze large volumes of text data, extract meaningful patterns, and inform decision-making. Explore techniques such as sentiment analysis and topic modeling, gaining a deeper understanding of how text mining can be a valuable asset in a data-driven business landscape.

Charting Your Course: Strategies for Continued Mastery

As you conclude this chapter and the book, consider the ways in which you can continue your journey of mastery in R programming. The field is dynamic, with new packages, techniques, and applications emerging regularly. Equip yourself with strategies that ensure your skills remain sharp and adaptable.

Lifelong Learning in R

Recognize that learning in the world of R programming is a continual process. Stay abreast of developments in the R community, engage with online forums, and participate in collaborative projects. Leverage platforms such as GitHub to explore open-source projects, contribute to the community, and learn from the collective wisdom of R practitioners worldwide.

Specialization and Depth

Consider the possibility of specialization within the R ecosystem. Whether it's becoming an expert in a specific package, diving deeper into statistical modeling, or exploring advanced machine learning techniques, specializing can enhance your value in a particular domain. Balance breadth with depth to develop a well-rounded skill set.

Building a Professional Portfolio

Craft a professional portfolio showcasing your R programming skills. Share your projects, case studies, and any contributions to the R community. A well-curated portfolio serves not only as a testament to your capabilities but also as a valuable resource when seeking employment opportunities or collaborating on projects with peers.

Mentorship and Collaboration

Consider the benefits of mentorship and collaboration. Engage with experienced R programmers, seek guidance, and participate in collaborative projects. Learning from others' experiences can provide valuable insights and shortcuts, accelerating your learning curve. Additionally, collaboration exposes you to diverse perspectives and approaches.

Conclusion

As you wrap up this capstone chapter, celebrate the journey you've undertaken in mastering R programming. Reflect on the challenges you've overcome, the skills you've acquired, and the practical applications you've explored. Armed with a comprehensive understanding of R, you're not just a coder;

you're a problem solver equipped to tackle real-world challenges.

The journey doesn't end here. Embrace the mindset of continuous learning, stay curious, and adapt to the evolving landscape of data science and programming. Your proficiency in R is not just a skill; it's a gateway to a world of possibilities. May your future endeavors in the realm of R programming be as rewarding as the journey that brought you to this point.

Chapter 8: Renaissance of R Packages

Welcome to the vibrant world of R packages, where a vast collection of specialized tools empowers data scientists and enthusiasts to tackle diverse data-driven tasks. In this chapter, we embark on a journey to explore the renaissance of R packages, witnessing their transformative impact on data analysis, visualization, and statistical modeling.

R packages, the building blocks of the R ecosystem, have revolutionized the way we interact with data. They provide a modular, extensible, and collaborative platform for developing and sharing innovative data science solutions. From data manipulation and visualization to machine learning and statistical modeling, R packages offer a wealth of specialized tools that cater to the ever-evolving needs of data practitioners.

The renaissance of R packages is driven by several factors:

- The growing demand for data-driven insights across diverse industries: Businesses, organizations, and researchers are increasingly relying on data to inform decision-making, leading to a surge in demand for tools that can effectively extract insights from data.

- The democratization of data science: With the increasing availability of data and computational resources, data science is becoming more accessible to a wider range of individuals, fostering a vibrant community of R package developers and users.

- The continuous evolution of data science methodologies: As data science techniques and algorithms advance, R packages play a crucial role in translating these advancements into practical tools that can be readily used by data scientists.

The renaissance of R packages has transformed the data science landscape, enabling data practitioners to:

- Tackle complex data analysis tasks efficiently: R packages provide a rich toolbox for manipulating, analyzing, and visualizing data, streamlining the entire data science workflow.

- Create captivating data visualizations: R packages offer a comprehensive collection of visualization tools, enabling data scientists to create informative and aesthetically pleasing visualizations that communicate insights effectively.

- Develop and apply sophisticated statistical models: R packages provide a vast array of statistical modeling tools, allowing data scientists to build robust and reliable models that extract meaningful patterns from data.

- Share and collaborate on data science solutions: R packages promote collaboration and knowledge sharing within the data science community, enabling researchers and practitioners to build upon each other's work and accelerate innovation.

The thriving ecosystem of R packages continues to grow and evolve, providing data scientists with an ever-expanding arsenal of tools to tackle the challenges of the data-driven world. As we delve deeper into the world of R packages, we will uncover the transformative power of these specialized tools and explore their impact on shaping the future of data science.

Navigating the Sea of R Packages

The vast collection of R packages, while offering immense power and versatility, can sometimes pose a challenge to navigate. With thousands of packages available, finding the right tools for a specific task can be overwhelming. To effectively navigate this sea of packages, consider the following strategies:

- Identify the task at hand: Clearly define the data analysis, visualization, or modeling task you want to accomplish. This will help narrow down your search and focus on packages relevant to your specific needs.

- Utilize search engines and package repositories: Online resources like CRAN (Comprehensive R Archive Network) and RStudio's package manager provide comprehensive listings and search functionalities to find packages matching your keywords or tasks.

- Explore package documentation and examples: Before installing a package, thoroughly review its documentation, including its functions, usage examples, and vignettes. This will provide insights into the package's capabilities and suitability for your task.

- Consult user reviews and community forums: Online communities, such as R-help and Stack Overflow, offer valuable feedback and discussions about R packages. User reviews and discussions can provide insights into a package's performance, strengths, and potential limitations.

- Consider package dependencies: When selecting a package, be mindful of its dependencies, which are other packages required for its proper functioning. Ensure that you have the necessary dependencies installed before using the package.

- Stay updated with package updates: Regularly check for updates to the packages you use.

By employing these strategies, you can effectively navigate the vast sea of R packages, selecting the right tools to tackle your data science challenges and harness the power of this vibrant ecosystem to achieve your data-driven goals.

Gems Unearthed: Hidden Treasures in R's Package Repository

Within the vast repository of R packages lie hidden treasures, gems that offer unique capabilities and functionalities, often overlooked amidst the more popular and well-known packages. These gems can provide innovative solutions to specific data analysis tasks, enhance data visualization techniques, or introduce novel statistical modeling approaches.

To uncover these hidden treasures, venture beyond the familiar and explore the lesser-known corners of the package repository. Engage with niche communities, participate in online discussions, and seek recommendations from experienced data scientists. With an open mind and a willingness to explore, you may discover invaluable tools that can transform your data science workflow.

Here are a few examples of hidden gems worth exploring:

data.table: An incredibly fast and efficient data manipulation package, offering superior performance over base R data frames and providing a wide range of flexible data management tools.

ggplot2: A powerful and versatile data visualization package, known for its aesthetic and customizable plots, enabling data scientists to create informative and visually appealing visualizations.

caret: A comprehensive toolkit for training, tuning, and evaluating machine learning models, providing a streamlined process for developing and optimizing predictive models.

tidyverse: A collection of packages that share a consistent design philosophy, grammar, and data structures, promoting a unified and cohesive data science workflow.

shiny: An innovative package for creating interactive web applications directly from R, enabling data scientists to share their insights and analyses with a wider audience in a dynamic and engaging manner.

These are just a few examples of the hidden treasures that lie within R's package repository. By venturing beyond the well-trodden paths and exploring the lesser-known corners of the package ecosystem, you may uncover gems that can revolutionize your data science endeavors and propel your data-driven insights to new heights.

Crafting Your Signature: Building and Sharing R Packages

The world of R packages is not just about consuming and utilizing existing tools; it also presents an exciting opportunity to create and share your own signature packages. By developing your own packages, you can contribute to the growing ecosystem of data science tools, address specific challenges in your domain, and showcase your expertise and innovation.

Building an R Package

From Idea to Implementation

Transforming your ideas into a functional R package involves a structured process:

1. Concept Development: Clearly define the purpose and functionality of your package. Identify the problems it solves, the target audience, and the unique contributions it makes to the data science landscape.

2. Code Design and Implementation: Write clean, well-documented code that adheres to R programming best practices. Utilize modularity, testing, and documentation to ensure the package's functionality, maintainability, and usability.

3. Package Structure and Organization: Structure your package following R package guidelines, including the creation of a DESCRIPTION file, a NAMESPACE file, and appropriate directory structure.

4. Package Testing and Validation: Rigorously test your package using various testing frameworks, ensuring it functions as intended and handles various data types and scenarios.

5. Documentation and User Experience: Provide comprehensive documentation, including function descriptions, usage examples, and vignettes, to guide users in effectively utilizing your package.

Sharing Your R Package: From Local to Global

Once your package is ready to share, follow these steps to make it accessible to the wider R community:

1. Create a GitHub Repository: Establish a GitHub repository to store your package code, documentation, and version control history.

2. Package Submission to CRAN: Submit your package to CRAN, the official repository of R packages, for review and consideration for inclusion.

3. Package Publication and Dissemination: Once accepted, your package will be available for installation through CRAN and other package repositories. Promote your package through online communities, forums, and publications.

Benefits of Sharing Your R Package

Sharing your R package offers several benefits:

- Contribution to the Data Science Community: Your package expands the data science toolkit, providing valuable tools for others to address their data-driven challenges.

- Recognition and Reputation: Showcase your expertise and innovation, gaining recognition within the data science community.

- Feedback and Collaboration: Seek and receive feedback from users, leading to improvements and new features.

- Potential for Impact: Your package can be adopted by organizations and researchers, making a real-world impact on data-driven decision-making.

By crafting and sharing your R packages, you leave your mark on the data science landscape, contributing to a collaborative ecosystem that drives innovation and empowers data-driven solutions.

Chapter 9: Optimizing Performance: R's Speed and Efficiency Secrets

As a data scientist, you are constantly working with large datasets, complex models, and time-consuming computations. While R is a powerful tool for data analysis and machine learning, it's also important to be aware of some optimization techniques to ensure that your code is running as efficiently as possible. In this chapter, you will unlock the secrets to R's speed and efficiency, enabling you to tackle even the most demanding tasks with ease.

Turbocharge Your Code:

Strategies for Optimizing R Performance

In the realm of data science, time is a valuable commodity, and efficient code execution is paramount. R, while a versatile language, can sometimes suffer from performance bottlenecks, especially when dealing with large datasets or complex computations. To unleash the true power of R and transform your data science workflow, mastering optimization techniques is essential.

Embracing Vectorization:

The Power of Parallel Processing

Vectorization, the fundamental principle of R programming, involves applying operations to entire vectors or matrices instead of looping over individual elements. This approach harnesses the power of parallel processing, significantly improving computational efficiency. For instance, using vectorized functions like rowSums() and colSums() for matrix operations is far more efficient than using explicit loops.

Data Structure Selection: Choosing the Right Tool for the Job

Data frames, while versatile, may not always be the most efficient choice for large datasets. Consider using matrices or lists for specific tasks, as they offer faster access and manipulation capabilities.

Memory Management: Avoiding Unnecessary Data Storage

Excessive memory consumption can hinder performance. Utilize techniques like garbage collection and memory profiling to identify and eliminate memory leaks. Regularly free up unused memory to ensure efficient resource utilization.

Code Profiling: Unveiling Performance Bottlenecks

Code profiling involves identifying the most time-consuming parts of your code. Tools like rprof() and microbenchmark() provide insights into code execution time, allowing you to target specific areas for optimization.

Precompiled Packages: Leveraging Compiled Code for Speed

Precompiled packages, such as dplyr and data.table, offer significant performance gains by converting R code into native machine code. Utilize these packages for tasks like data manipulation and analysis to achieve faster execution times.

Parallel Computing: Unleashing the Power of Multiple Cores

Parallel computing frameworks, such as parallel and doParallel, enable you to distribute computations across multiple cores, significantly reducing processing time for large tasks. This approach is particularly beneficial for machine learning and statistical modeling.

Cloud-Based Solutions

Scalability for Massive Datasets

Cloud-based R solutions, such as Amazon SageMaker and Google Cloud AI Platform, provide scalable computing resources and pre-built tools for R-based data science. These platforms enable you to tackle massive datasets without the limitations of local hardware.

Continuous Code Refactoring: Maintaining Efficient Code Practices

Regularly review and refactor your code to eliminate inefficiencies and maintain optimal performance. Prioritize code clarity, modularity, and adherence to best practices to ensure long-term maintainability and efficiency.

By adopting these optimization strategies, you can transform your R code into a high-performance engine, capable of handling even the most demanding data analysis and machine learning tasks. As you continue to master these techniques, you will unlock the true potential of R and become a data scientist who can extract insights and build models with unparalleled efficiency.

Code Elegance:

Writing Efficient and Readable R Programs

In the pursuit of mastery in R programming, it is essential to not only produce functional code but also to prioritize code elegance. Writing efficient and readable R programs not only enhances collaboration and maintainability but also reflects a deeper understanding of the language. This subsection explores key principles and practices for achieving code elegance in your R projects.

Consistent Formatting and Style

Consistency in code formatting and style is crucial for readability. Adhering to a consistent coding style, whether it's spacing, indentation, or naming conventions, makes your code more accessible to others and, importantly, to your future self. Consider adopting popular style guides such as the tidyverse style guide or the Google R Style Guide.

Meaningful Variable and Function Names

Choosing descriptive names for variables and functions is fundamental to code readability. Aim for clarity and conciseness when naming your entities, making it easier for others (and yourself) to understand the purpose and functionality of each component. Avoid overly cryptic or abbreviated names, favoring explicitness.

Commenting for Clarity

While it's crucial to write code that is self-explanatory, judicious use of comments can provide additional context or explanations for complex sections. Comment sparingly, focusing on areas where the code's intention may not be immediately evident. Well-placed comments can be invaluable for collaborators or when returning to your code after an extended period.

Modularization and Functions

Break down complex tasks into modular functions, each responsible for a specific subtask.. When designing functions, adhere to the principle of doing one thing well. Functions should have clear inputs, outputs, and a well-defined purpose, contributing to the overall clarity of your code.

Efficient Data Manipulation and Vectorization

R is optimized for vectorized operations, and leveraging this feature can significantly enhance code efficiency. When working with data, strive to use vectorized operations and functions instead of loops. This not only improves execution speed but also contributes to more concise and readable code.

Error Handling and Robustness

Account for potential errors in your code by implementing robust error handling. Use appropriate error messages and consider scenarios where your code might fail. Robust error handling not only makes your code more reliable but also aids in troubleshooting and debugging.

Version Control and Documentation

Incorporate version control tools like Git into your workflow to track changes and collaborate effectively. Regularly commit your code, providing meaningful commit messages. Additionally, maintain comprehensive documentation, including a README file, to guide users and collaborators through your project's structure, dependencies, and usage.

Continuous Learning and Code Reviews

Stay engaged with the R community, and actively participate in code reviews. Embrace feedback from peers, as it is a valuable opportunity to enhance your coding practices. Continuous learning and exposure to diverse coding styles contribute to the refinement of your own approach to writing elegant and efficient R programs.

By prioritizing code elegance in your R programming endeavors, you not only enhance the quality of your projects but also contribute to a culture of excellence within the broader R community. Strive for code that is not just functional but also a pleasure to read and maintain.

Debugging Like a Pro: Troubleshooting in R

Mastering the art of debugging is a crucial skill for any R programmer. This subsection equips you with effective strategies and tools to identify and resolve issues in your code. By honing your debugging skills, you'll not only overcome challenges more efficiently but also gain a deeper understanding of R's inner workings.

Understanding Error Messages

Error messages are your code's way of communicating issues. Learning to decipher these messages is a fundamental step in debugging. Let's explore common error types:

1. **Syntax Errors:**

```
1   # Example of a syntax error print("Hello, world!"
```

Syntax errors are straightforward—they indicate a violation of R's grammar rules. In this case, a missing parenthesis causes a syntax error.

2. **Runtime Errors:**

```
1    # Example of a runtime error x <- "5" y <- 2 z <- x + y
```

Runtime errors occur during code execution. Here, attempting to add a character ("5") to a numeric value (2) results in an error.

3. **Logical Errors:**

```
1    # Example of a logical error radius <- 3 area <- 2 * pi * radius
```

Logical errors don't produce immediate errors but lead to incorrect results. In this case, the formula for calculating the area of a circle is incorrect.

Print Statements and Visualization

Strategically placing print statements in your code helps trace its execution and inspect variable values at specific points. For example:

```
1    # Return print statements for debugging x <- 2 print("Before addition:")
5    print(x) x <- x + 3 print("After addition:") print(x)
```

You can also utilize visualization tools, such as plotting intermediate results or displaying dataframes, to gain insights into your code's behavior.

Interactive Debugging with browser()

The **browser()** function allows you to interactively explore your code at a specific point. Insert **browser()** where you suspect issues:

```
1   # Using browser() for interactive debugging calculate_area
2   <- function(radius) { diameter <- radius * 2 browser() area <- pi *
3   (radius^2) return(area) } result <- calculate_area(3)
```

When the function is called, it pauses at **browser()**, enabling you to inspect variables, run code interactively, and identify problems.

Utilizing RStudio's Debugging Tools

RStudio provides a robust set of debugging tools. Use breakpoints, step-through execution, and inspect variable values in the "Debug" tab. The following example showcases the use of breakpoints:

1. Place a breakpoint by clicking to the left of the line number.

2. Run the code in debug mode (**Debug > On Error** or **Ctrl + Shift + D**).

3. Execution pauses at the breakpoint, allowing you to analyze variables and step through code.

```
1    # Example using breakpoints in RStudio
2    x <- 5 y <- 3 z <- x + y # Place breakpoint here
```

Exception Handling with tryCatch()

Anticipate and handle errors gracefully using **tryCatch()**. This function allows you to define actions for different conditions, enhancing your code's robustness.

```
1    # Using tryCatch() for exception handling result <- tryCatch( expr =
2    { # Code that might cause an error result <- 10 / 0 },
3    error = function(e) { # Actions to take when an error occurs print
4    (paste("Error:", e$message)) result <- NA } )
```

Learning by Doing

The best way to master debugging is through hands-on experience. Apply the concepts discussed in this subsection to the case studies introduced earlier. Experiment with intentionally introducing errors and practice using various debugging techniques to identify and resolve them. Through practical application, you'll refine your troubleshooting skills and gain confidence in handling real-world challenges.

Remember, becoming proficient at debugging takes time and practice. As you encounter issues in your R projects, view them as valuable opportunities to enhance your skills. The ability to debug effectively is a hallmark of a seasoned R programmer, and by actively engaging with the debugging process, you'll accelerate your journey toward mastery.

Chapter 10: Ethical Data Science Practices in R

In the ever-expanding realm of data science, ethical considerations are paramount. As data scientists harness the power of R to extract insights from data, it becomes imperative to navigate the ethical landscape with diligence and responsibility. This chapter delves into the multifaceted realm of ethical data science practices, focusing on how R programming can be wielded to ensure integrity, transparency, and fairness in the utilization of data.

As we explore this chapter, we will navigate through key ethical principles that underpin responsible data science. From ensuring data privacy and security to addressing bias and discrimination, each section of this chapter serves as a guide to cultivating a conscientious and ethical approach to data science within the context of R programming.

Data, as a raw material for insights, holds immense power and potential. However, it is crucial to wield this power ethically, acknowledging the impact that data-driven decisions can have on individuals, communities, and society at large. Whether you are a seasoned data scientist or a newcomer to the field, this chapter provides valuable insights and practical strategies for integrating ethical considerations seamlessly into your R-based data science workflows.

As we embark on this exploration of ethical data science practices in R, let us collectively engage with the responsibility that comes with leveraging data as a tool for innovation and informed decision-making. Through an ethical lens, we can not only unlock the true potential of R programming but also contribute to a data-driven future that is fair, just, and respectful of the diverse perspectives and values that shape our world.

The Ethical Compass in Data Science

Data science, with its transformative capabilities, holds the potential to revolutionize industries, inform decision-making, and drive societal progress. However, this potential comes with a profound responsibility—the responsibility to navigate the ethical landscape that underlies the data-driven journey. In this section, we embark on a comprehensive exploration of the ethical considerations that guide responsible data science practices within the framework of R programming.

Understanding Ethical Data Science

The Intersection of Data and Ethics

Ethics in data science is not an afterthought; it is an integral part of the entire process—from data collection to analysis and interpretation. At its core, ethical data science involves making decisions that are just, fair, and considerate of the impact on individuals and communities. It goes beyond the technicalities of code and algorithms, extending into the realm of social responsibility.

Ethical Principles in Data Science

Several key ethical principles guide data scientists in their work. These principles include:

1. **Transparency:** Transparent practices involve clearly communicating the methods, sources, and limitations of data science processes. In R programming, this might manifest as well-documented code, explicit explanations of data preprocessing steps, and detailed descriptions of modeling choices.

2. **Fairness:** Ensuring fairness involves avoiding biases in data and models. In R, it requires vigilant scrutiny of algorithms and methodologies to identify and mitigate biases that may arise during data processing or model training.

3. **Privacy:** Respecting privacy is fundamental. R programming facilitates privacy-preserving techniques, such as anonymization and encryption, to safeguard individual data.

4. **Accountability:** Being accountable means taking responsibility for the consequences of data science actions. In R, this involves thorough testing, validation, and documenting assumptions to create a robust and accountable workflow.

5. **Integrity:** Upholding integrity involves maintaining honesty and truthfulness throughout the data science process. In R, this might include transparent reporting of results, acknowledging limitations, and avoiding cherry-picking favorable outcomes.

6. **Inclusivity:** Embracing inclusivity means considering diverse perspectives and ensuring that the benefits of data science are accessible to all. In R, this can be achieved by validating models across diverse datasets and populations.

Ethical Dilemmas in Data Science

Navigating ethical terrain often involves confronting dilemmas. Common ethical challenges in data science include:

1. **Bias and Discrimination:** Addressing bias and discrimination is a persistent challenge. In R, understanding and mitigating biases in algorithms, especially in machine learning models, is crucial for fostering fairness.

2. **Informed Consent:** Obtaining informed consent from individuals whose data is used is an ethical imperative. In R, mechanisms for obtaining and documenting consent can be integrated into the data collection and analysis pipeline.

3. **Data Ownership and Stewardship:** Determining who owns and stewards the data raises ethical questions. R provides tools for secure data handling, ensuring responsible practices in data ownership and stewardship.

4. **Data Security:** Safeguarding data against unauthorized access is essential. In R, encryption, secure coding practices, and regular security audits contribute to maintaining robust data security.

Applying Ethical Data Science in R

Data Collection and Preprocessing

Transparent Data Collection

Transparent data collection involves clearly documenting the sources, methods, and purposes of data collection. In R, this is achieved through detailed comments in code, metadata documentation, and comprehensive README files accompanying datasets.

Example:

```
1    # Data collection script # Source: XYZ Survey conducted in 2022
2    # Purpose: To analyze trends in consumer preferences
3    # Load necessary libraries library(dplyr)
4    # Read raw data raw_data <- read.csv("survey_data.csv")
5    # Data preprocessing steps # ...
```

Bias Mitigation in Data Preprocessing

Addressing biases during data preprocessing is crucial for fair analyses. In R, tools like the **tidyverse** package offer functions for exploring and transforming data, allowing for careful examination and correction of biases.

Example:

```
1  # Bias mitigation in data preprocessing
2  # Identify and address gender bias in the dataset cleaned_data
3  <- raw_data %>% mutate(gender = recode(gender,
4  "F" = "Female", "M" = "Male", "O" = "Other"))
```

Model Development and Evaluation

Fairness Assessment in Models

Ensuring fairness in models requires ongoing assessment and adjustment. In R, fairness metrics and visualization tools can be integrated into the model development process to identify and rectify disparities.

Example:

R code

```
1  # Assessing fairness in a predictive model
2  # Using fairness metrics from the 'fair' package library(fair)
3  model <- glm(outcome ~ features, data = training_data, family = "binomial")
4  # Assess fairness fairness_report <- assess_fairness(model,
5  data = validation_data) print(fairness_report)
```

Documentation of Model Choices and Assumptions

Transparent reporting of model choices and assumptions contributes to accountability. In R, comprehensive documentation, including markdown files or R notebooks, aids in conveying the rationale behind modeling decisions.

Example:

83

R code

```
1    # Model documentation # Model: Random Forest Classifier
2    # Purpose: Predicting customer churn # Features:
3    Age, Monthly Spend, Customer Satisfaction
4    # Hyperparameters: n_estimators = 100,
5    max_depth = 10 # Model training code # ...
```

Interpretation and Communication of Results

Transparent Reporting

Transparent reporting involves clearly articulating the results, including uncertainties and limitations. R facilitates transparent reporting through R Markdown documents or Jupyter notebooks that weave together code, results, and commentary.

Example:

R code

```
1    # Transparent reporting using R Markdown --- title:
2    "Analysis of Customer Churn" author:
3    "Data Scientist" date: "2023-11-01" output: html_document ---
4    # Introduction This analysis explores factors influencing customer churn...
5    # Model Results The Random Forest model achieved an accuracy of 85%...
6    # Conclusion In conclusion,
7    while the model shows promising results...
```

Addressing Stakeholder Concerns

Being responsive to stakeholder concerns is a part of ethical communication. In R, interactive visualizations and dashboards can be created using packages like **shiny** to allow stakeholders to explore data and results actively.

Example:

R code

```
1   # Interactive dashboard using shiny library(shiny)
2   # Define UI ui <- fluidPage( titlePanel("Customer Churn Analysis"),
3   sidebarLayout( sidebarPanel( # User inputs and controls ), mainPanel(
4       # Interactive visualizations ) ) ) # Define server server
5       <- function(input, output) { # Server logic for interactive elements }
6   # Run the Shiny app shinyApp(ui, server)
```

Emerging Technologies and Ethical Considerations

Responsible AI and Machine Learning

Explainable AI

Incorporating explainable AI practices ensures that machine learning models provide understandable and interpretable results. In R, packages like **lime** and **DALEX** enable model interpretation and explainability.

Example:

R code

```
1   # Explainable AI using DALEX library(DALEX)
2   # Create an explainer explainer
3   <- explain(model, data = validation_data, y = validation_data$outcome) #
```

Navigating the Regulatory Landscape

In the rapidly evolving field of data science, navigating the regulatory landscape is crucial to ensure ethical and legal compliance. As data scientists utilize R programming to extract insights and make informed decisions, they must be cognizant of the regulations that govern the collection, processing, and use of data. This subsection explores key considerations and strategies for navigating the regulatory landscape in the context of ethical data science practices.

Data Protection Regulations

General Data Protection Regulation (GDPR)

The GDPR, implemented in the European Union, sets stringent standards for the protection of personal data. It applies to any organization processing the personal data of EU residents. Data scientists using R programming should be aware of GDPR principles, such as the right to be forgotten, data minimization, and the requirement for explicit consent.

Example:

RCopy code

```
# Anonymizing data to comply with GDPR anon_data <-
raw_data %>% select(-c("name", "email")) %>% mutate(id =
row_number())
```

California Consumer Privacy Act (CCPA)

The CCPA is a comprehensive privacy law in California,
granting consumers certain rights regarding their personal
information. Data scientists working with data from California
residents using R should be mindful of CCPA requirements,
such as the right to know and the right to opt-out of data
sales.

Example:

RCopy code

```
# Complying with CCPA data access request user_data <-
raw_data %>% filter(user_id == requested_user_id) %>%
select(-c("social_security_number", "credit_card_number"))
```

Industry-Specific Regulations

Health Insurance Portability and Accountability Act (HIPAA)

In the healthcare sector, the HIPAA regulates the use and
disclosure of protected health information (PHI). Data scientists
handling health-related data with R must adhere to HIPAA

standards, ensuring the secure handling of PHI and implementing necessary safeguards.

Example:

RCopy code

```
# HIPAA-compliant data processing hipaa_compliant_data <-
health_data %>% filter(!is.na(patient_id)) %>% select(-
c("diagnosis_code", "patient_notes"))
```

Financial Industry Regulatory Authority (FINRA)

For data scientists working with financial data, adherence to FINRA regulations is critical. FINRA sets guidelines for data protection and ethical considerations within the financial industry. Data scientists utilizing R in this context should ensure compliance with these regulations.

Example:

RCopy code

```
# Ensuring compliance with FINRA data handling financial_data
<- read.csv("financial_data.csv") # Implement necessary data
access controls and encryption
```

Ethical and Regulatory Documentation

Data Impact Assessments

Conducting data impact assessments is a proactive approach to ensure compliance with regulations and ethical standards. R programming facilitates the documentation of data impact assessments, including identifying potential risks and outlining mitigation strategies.

Example:

RCopy code

```
# Data impact assessment template using R Markdown --- title: "Data Impact Assessment" author: "Data Scientist" date: "2023-11-15" output: pdf_document --- # Executive Summary ... # Assessment Findings ... # Mitigation Strategies ...
```

Compliance Audits

Regular compliance audits are essential to verify that data science practices align with regulatory requirements. In R, automated scripts and reports can be created to facilitate compliance audits, ensuring that data processing activities adhere to ethical and legal standards.

Example:

RCopy code

```r
# Automated compliance audit script # Check data processing
activities against regulatory requirements
check_gdpr_compliance <- function(data) { # Check for
explicit consent if (!all(data$consent == "explicit")) {
warning("Data processing lacks explicit consent.") } #
Additional checks... } # Run compliance checks on the dataset
check_gdpr_compliance(raw_data)
```

Collaborating with Legal Experts

Given the complexity of data protection regulations and the
dynamic nature of the legal landscape, collaborating with legal
experts is invaluable. Data scientists using R programming
should establish communication channels with legal
professionals within their organizations to ensure ongoing
compliance and ethical data science practices.

Example:

RCopy code

```r
# Collaboration with legal experts # Regular consultations with
legal team to review data practices legal_review <-
function(data_practices) { # Legal review and
recommendations } # Example usage
legal_review(data_practices)
```

Navigating the regulatory landscape is an integral component of ethical data science practices in R programming. As data scientists, it is imperative to stay informed about existing and emerging regulations, ensuring that data collection, processing, and analysis align with legal and ethical standards. By integrating regulatory considerations into the data science workflow, professionals can contribute to a trustworthy and responsible use of data, fostering public trust and safeguarding individual privacy and rights.

Building Responsible Models: Fairness and Bias Mitigation

As data scientists utilize R programming to construct models that inform decision-making, it becomes paramount to address the ethical considerations surrounding fairness and bias mitigation. The development of responsible models involves not only achieving high predictive accuracy but also ensuring that the impact of these models is equitable across diverse populations. In this subsection, we explore strategies for building models that prioritize fairness and mitigate biases.

Understanding Bias in Models

Types of Bias

91

Bias can manifest in various forms throughout the data science process, from data collection to model training and deployment. Understanding the types of bias, including selection bias, measurement bias, and algorithmic bias, is fundamental to identifying and mitigating its impact.

Impact of Bias

Bias in models can lead to unfair and discriminatory outcomes. It may result in unequal treatment of different groups, reinforcing existing disparities, and perpetuating systemic inequities. Recognizing the potential consequences of biased models is crucial for ethical data science practices.

Mitigating Bias in Model Development

Diverse and Representative Data

The foundation for mitigating bias lies in the data used to train models. Ensuring that datasets are diverse and representative of the populations they aim to serve helps reduce the risk of biased model outcomes. In R programming, exploratory data analysis and visualization can assist in understanding the demographic composition of the data.

Fair Model Development Practices

Incorporating fairness considerations during the model development process is essential. This involves assessing the impact of different features on model outcomes, identifying potential sources of bias, and implementing adjustments to promote fairness. Various fairness metrics and techniques can be applied using R packages designed for bias mitigation.

Model Evaluation and Validation

Rigorous Testing

Thoroughly evaluating models for fairness and bias requires rigorous testing. Utilizing testing datasets that represent diverse groups and scenarios helps uncover potential biases that may have been introduced during model development. Rigorous testing involves assessing performance across subgroups to ensure equitable outcomes.

Continuous Monitoring

Model fairness is not a one-time consideration; it requires continuous monitoring. As new data becomes available and societal dynamics evolve, models must be reevaluated to detect and address emerging biases. Incorporating automated monitoring processes using R scripts facilitates ongoing assessments.

Ethical Considerations in Model Deployment

Transparency and Explainability

Transparent model deployment involves clearly communicating how a model works, the variables it considers, and the rationale behind its predictions. In R, creating comprehensive documentation and leveraging explainability tools enhances transparency, enabling stakeholders to understand and trust the model.

User Feedback and Iterative Improvement

Promoting user feedback and iterative improvement is a key component of responsible model deployment. By engaging with end-users and stakeholders, data scientists can gain insights into the real-world impact of models, identify unintended consequences, and iteratively refine models to enhance fairness.

Closing Out the Chapter

In closing this chapter on ethical data science practices in R, it is essential to recognize that building responsible models extends beyond technical proficiency. It involves a commitment to ongoing learning, collaboration with diverse stakeholders, and a dedication to addressing the societal implications of data-driven decision-making.

As data scientists, embracing ethical considerations in model development is not only a professional responsibility but a moral imperative. The choices made in the construction and deployment of models have far-reaching consequences, influencing individuals, communities, and society at large. By conscientiously incorporating fairness and bias mitigation strategies into the fabric of R-based data science workflows, professionals can contribute to a more equitable and ethical data landscape.

In the ever-evolving field of data science, where technological advancements continue to shape the way we interact with data, ethical considerations must remain at the forefront. This chapter serves as a guide and a call to action, encouraging data scientists to navigate the complexities of ethical model development in R with diligence, empathy, and a commitment to building a more just and inclusive data-driven future.

Chapter 11: Mastering the Art of R Reporting

In the dynamic landscape of data science, the ability to communicate findings effectively is as crucial as the technical skills employed in analysis. Chapter 11 invites you into the realm of mastering the art of R reporting—an integral facet of the data scientist's toolkit. As you delve into this chapter, you will embark on a journey that transcends raw data and code, exploring how R can be harnessed to create compelling, informative, and visually engaging reports.

Effective reporting in R is not merely a presentation of results; it is a story crafted with data, insights, and visualizations. Whether you are communicating with colleagues, stakeholders, or the broader public, the skills acquired in this chapter will empower you to convey complex information with clarity and impact.

From the fundamentals of R Markdown to advanced techniques in data visualization and interactive reporting, this chapter unfolds a rich tapestry of tools and strategies. As you navigate through each section, you will discover how to seamlessly integrate code, narrative, and visual elements to produce reports that transcend the boundaries of mere documentation.

Whether you are a seasoned R programmer or just beginning your journey, mastering the art of R reporting is a skill set that transcends technical proficiency. It transforms your ability to tell a compelling data-driven story, allowing you to share insights, facilitate decision-making, and contribute meaningfully to the wider discourse of data science.

Join us in unraveling the intricacies of R reporting, where the fusion of code and creativity converges to elevate your communication skills. This chapter is your guide to not only mastering the tools and techniques but also developing an intuitive sense of storytelling with data. Let the exploration begin as we unlock the full potential of R for creating impactful and influential reports.

Dynamic Reporting with R Markdown

In the realm of R programming, the power to seamlessly integrate code, narrative, and visualizations into a cohesive and dynamic document lies within the realm of R Markdown. This section explores the art of dynamic reporting, where R Markdown serves as the canvas upon which data-driven stories come to life.

Unveiling the Potential of R Markdown

The R Markdown Framework

R Markdown is more than just a document format; it is a flexible framework that allows data scientists to create reports that evolve alongside their analyses. Whether you are generating a one-time summary or crafting a document designed to update dynamically with changing data, R Markdown provides the structure and flexibility to bring your narratives to life.

Integrating Code and Narrative

One of the hallmarks of dynamic reporting with R Markdown is the seamless integration of code and narrative. By interleaving code chunks with explanatory text, you create a comprehensive document that not only communicates your findings but also provides a transparent and reproducible record of your analysis process.

R Markdown Document Structure

Understanding the structure of an R Markdown document is fundamental to leveraging its dynamic capabilities. From YAML metadata to markdown content and embedded code chunks, each element plays a role in shaping the final output. As you explore dynamic reporting, you'll learn to harness the full potential of R Markdown's structure.

Dynamic Elements in R Markdown

Parameters and Customization

R Markdown supports parameterization, allowing you to create reports that adapt to different scenarios or datasets. Learn how to utilize parameters to customize your reports dynamically, providing users with the flexibility to explore various aspects of the data or analysis.

Conditional Rendering

Take dynamic reporting to the next level by incorporating conditional rendering. With conditional statements in R Markdown, you can control which sections, visualizations, or insights are displayed based on specified conditions. This allows you to create reports that cater to different audiences or emphasize particular aspects depending on the context.

Iterative Reporting with Loops

Harness the power of loops within R Markdown to iterate over data, analyses, or visualizations. This dynamic approach enables you to create reports that adapt to changes in data structure or size, providing a scalable solution for presenting insights from diverse datasets.

Advanced Visualizations and Interactivity

Interactive Dashboards

Elevate your dynamic reporting by integrating interactive dashboards into R Markdown documents. Learn how to utilize packages like **shiny** to create dashboards that allow users to explore data, adjust parameters, and interact with visualizations, all within the context of a dynamic report.

Embedding HTML Widgets

Explore the integration of HTML widgets into R Markdown documents to enhance visualizations with interactive elements. From dynamic charts to interactive maps, HTML widgets provide a dynamic layer to engage users and convey complex insights in an accessible manner.

Collaboration and Reproducibility

Version Control and Collaboration

Discover best practices for version control and collaboration within the context of dynamic reporting. Learn how to leverage tools like Git and GitHub to manage changes, collaborate with team members, and maintain a versioned history of your dynamic reports.

Reproducibility and Documentation

Dynamic reporting with R Markdown inherently promotes reproducibility. Understand how to document your R Markdown workflow, including session information, package versions, and dependencies, to ensure that your dynamic reports remain reproducible across different environments.

Closing Thoughts on Dynamic Reporting

As you delve into the intricacies of dynamic reporting with R Markdown, you'll not only acquire technical skills but also cultivate a mindset of effective communication and collaboration. Dynamic reporting transcends static documents, providing a platform for data-driven narratives that evolve with the ever-changing landscape of data science.

This section serves as your guide to unlocking the full potential of R Markdown for dynamic reporting. Whether you are crafting interactive dashboards, adapting reports to changing data, or collaborating seamlessly with colleagues, the skills gained here will empower you to create reports that are not only informative but also agile and responsive to the dynamic nature of data science.

Crafting Engaging Reports: Beyond the Basics

In the ever-evolving landscape of data science, crafting engaging reports goes beyond the basics of data analysis and visualization. This section takes you on a journey beyond the fundamentals, exploring advanced techniques and strategies to elevate your reports from informative to truly captivating. Whether you are communicating with stakeholders, presenting findings to a broader audience, or simply aiming to make a lasting impact, mastering the art of crafting engaging reports is a skill set that transcends technical proficiency.

Narrative Flow and Storytelling

Creating a Compelling Storyline

Move beyond standalone visualizations and embrace the art of storytelling in your reports. Learn how to structure your narrative, guiding your audience through a coherent and compelling storyline that highlights key insights and findings. A well-crafted narrative flow not only enhances comprehension but also keeps your audience engaged from start to finish.

Incorporating Context and Background

Provide context and background information to give your audience a deeper understanding of the subject matter. By contextualizing your analysis within a broader framework, you create a narrative that is not only data-driven but also resonates with the larger story your data is telling.

Design Principles for Visual Impact

Advanced Data Visualization Techniques

Explore advanced data visualization techniques to add layers of depth and nuance to your reports. From interactive heatmaps to hierarchical visualizations, this section delves into innovative approaches that go beyond standard chart types. Learn how to choose the right visualization for your data and the story you want to tell.

Color Psychology and Accessibility

Master the art of color selection by understanding the principles of color psychology. Discover how the strategic use of color can evoke emotions, highlight key insights, and enhance the overall visual impact of your reports. Additionally, delve into considerations for accessibility, ensuring that your visualizations are inclusive and comprehensible to all audiences.

Dynamic and Interactive Elements

Incorporating Dynamic Elements

Take your reports to the next level by incorporating dynamic and interactive elements. From animated visualizations to interactive sliders and filters, learn how to create a user-friendly experience that allows your audience to engage with the data actively. Dynamic elements add a layer of sophistication and versatility to your reports, making them more memorable and impactful.

Responsive Design for Various Platforms

Craft reports that are not bound by a single platform. Explore responsive design principles to ensure that your reports adapt seamlessly to different devices and screen sizes. Whether viewed on a desktop, tablet, or smartphone, responsive design enhances accessibility and ensures a consistent and engaging user experience.

Collaborative and Iterative Reporting

Collaborative Editing and Feedback

Embrace collaborative reporting by leveraging tools that facilitate real-time editing and feedback. Learn how to use platforms that enable team members to collaborate seamlessly on a single report, providing valuable insights, suggestions, and improvements. Collaboration enhances the quality of your reports and fosters a culture of collective intelligence.

Iterative Reporting and Continuous Improvement

Recognize the importance of iterative reporting and continuous improvement. Understand how to gather feedback, analyze report performance, and iteratively refine your reports over time. By embracing an iterative approach, you ensure that your reports remain dynamic, relevant, and continuously enhance their impact.

Empathy in Communication

Understanding Your Audience

Go beyond data interpretation and analysis to truly understand your audience. Develop the ability to tailor your reports to the needs, interests, and level of expertise of your audience. By fostering empathy in your communication, you create reports that resonate with your audience on a deeper level.

Inclusive Language and Accessibility

Cultivate inclusive language in your reports, ensuring that your content is accessible and welcoming to a diverse audience. Learn about best practices for creating reports that are free from biases and that embrace inclusivity, fostering an environment where everyone can engage with the content without feeling excluded.

Mastering the Art of Engaging Reports

In conclusion, mastering the art of crafting engaging reports goes beyond technical proficiency; it requires a combination of narrative finesse, design acumen, and a deep understanding of your audience. This section equips you with advanced techniques and strategies to create reports that captivate, inspire, and leave a lasting impression.

As you venture into the realm of crafting engaging reports beyond the basics, remember that each report is an opportunity to tell a compelling story with your data. Whether you are presenting to colleagues, stakeholders, or the public, the skills acquired in this section will empower you to elevate your reports to new heights, making them not only informative but truly memorable.

Interactive Dashboards: Showcasing Your Data with Shiny

In the dynamic landscape of data communication, the ability to showcase your data interactively is a powerful skill that sets your reports apart. This section delves into the world of Shiny, an R package that empowers you to create interactive dashboards seamlessly integrated into your reports. From dynamic visualizations to user-friendly interfaces, Shiny transforms static reports into immersive, hands-on experiences that engage and captivate your audience.

Unveiling the Power of Shiny

Introduction to Shiny

Shiny is an R package that opens the door to a new dimension of data presentation. It enables the creation of web applications with interactive elements, allowing users to explore and interact with your data dynamically. This section provides an overview of Shiny's capabilities and sets the stage for diving into its powerful features.

The Shiny App Lifecycle

Understand the lifecycle of a Shiny app, from its creation to deployment. Explore the various components, including user interface (UI) elements and server logic, that come together to form an interactive Shiny application. Grasp the fundamentals of structuring your Shiny app for optimal performance and user experience.

Building Interactive Dashboards

Designing the User Interface (UI)

Learn the art of designing an intuitive and visually appealing user interface for your Shiny app. Explore the plethora of UI elements, such as sliders, buttons, and interactive plots, that can be seamlessly integrated. Master the principles of layout design to create a polished and engaging dashboard.

Implementing Server Logic

Delve into the server logic that powers your Shiny app. Understand how to incorporate R code that responds to user inputs, dynamically updates visualizations, and ensures a responsive and interactive user experience. Grasp the intricacies of reactive programming, a cornerstone of Shiny app development.

Advanced Features of Shiny

Customizing Themes and Styles

Elevate the aesthetics of your Shiny app by customizing themes and styles. Discover how to tailor the look and feel of your dashboard to align with your brand or storytelling narrative. From color schemes to font choices, customization adds a layer of professionalism and coherence to your interactive reports.

Incorporating Advanced Visualizations

Integrate advanced visualizations into your Shiny app to convey complex insights with clarity. Explore the use of interactive charts, maps, and plots that enhance the depth of your data storytelling. Leverage R packages designed for Shiny to unlock a rich array of visualization possibilities.

Deployment and Sharing

Hosting Shiny Apps

Navigate the process of deploying your Shiny app for wider accessibility. Learn about different hosting options, from deploying on Shiny Server to leveraging cloud platforms. Understand the considerations for choosing a hosting solution that aligns with your project's requirements and audience.

Sharing and Collaboration

Explore strategies for sharing and collaborating on your Shiny app. Whether sharing the app within your organization or with a broader audience, discover how to provide secure access and gather feedback. Learn about best practices for collaborative development to enhance the quality and impact of your Shiny dashboards.

Shiny and Reproducibility

Ensuring Reproducibility

Understand the importance of reproducibility in Shiny app development. Explore strategies for creating reproducible Shiny apps, including version control, documentation, and package management. By prioritizing reproducibility, you ensure that your interactive dashboards remain reliable and maintainable over time.

Incorporating R Markdown and Shiny

Uncover the seamless integration of R Markdown and Shiny, creating a harmonious blend of dynamic reporting and interactive dashboards. Learn how to embed Shiny apps within R Markdown documents, combining the strengths of both frameworks to produce comprehensive and engaging data narratives.

Conclusion: Elevating Your Reports with Shiny

In conclusion, the integration of Shiny into your data science toolkit opens up a realm of possibilities for creating interactive, engaging, and impactful reports. Shiny empowers you to move beyond static visualizations, providing a platform to showcase your data in a way that invites exploration and interaction.

As you embark on the journey of building interactive dashboards with Shiny, remember that the true power lies not just in the technology but in your ability to tell a compelling story with your data. This section equips you with the knowledge and skills to leverage Shiny effectively, transforming your reports into immersive experiences that captivate your audience and bring your data narratives to life.

Chapter 12: Security in Statistical Computing: Safeguarding Your R Environment

In the realm of statistical computing, where data serves as the lifeblood of analyses, safeguarding the integrity, confidentiality, and availability of your R environment is paramount. Chapter 12 delves into the crucial domain of security in statistical computing, equipping you with the knowledge and strategies to fortify your R ecosystem against potential threats.

As data scientists and statisticians navigate the landscape of R programming, they encounter a diverse array of challenges, from data breaches to unauthorized access and malicious attacks. This chapter serves as your guide to fortify your defenses, ensuring that your statistical computing endeavors remain resilient in the face of evolving security risks.

From securing sensitive data to implementing robust access controls and addressing potential vulnerabilities in your R code, each section of this chapter addresses key facets of security that are integral to responsible statistical computing. As you embark on this exploration of security measures in the R environment, you will gain insights into industry best practices, practical implementations, and emerging trends that shape the landscape of data security.

In an era where data is a valuable currency and the implications of security breaches reverberate across organizations and individuals, the importance of securing your statistical computing environment cannot be overstated. Join us in this chapter as we delve into the intricacies of security in statistical computing, arming you with the tools and knowledge needed to navigate the digital landscape with confidence and resilience.

Fortifying the Castle:

Security Measures in R Programming

In the ever-expanding digital landscape, fortifying your castle—your R programming environment—is a critical undertaking to ensure the safety and integrity of your statistical computing endeavors. This section explores essential security measures that form the bulwark against potential threats, safeguarding your data, code, and infrastructure from vulnerabilities and unauthorized access.

Understanding the Security Landscape

Identifying Security Risks in R Programming

Embark on a comprehensive exploration of the security risks inherent in the world of R programming. From data breaches to code vulnerabilities, understanding potential threats is the first step in crafting an effective defense strategy. This section provides insights into common security risks and their implications for statistical computing.

The Intersection of Data Privacy and Security

Recognize the inseparable link between data privacy and security. Delve into the principles and regulations governing data privacy, such as GDPR and HIPAA, and understand how they influence security considerations in R programming. Navigating this intersection is crucial for establishing a secure foundation for statistical computing.

Protecting Sensitive Data in R

Encryption and Secure Data Transmission

Explore the realm of encryption as a shield for sensitive data. Understand how to implement encryption measures within R to secure data transmission and storage. From SSL/TLS protocols to secure socket connections, discover techniques to safeguard the confidentiality of your data.

Anonymization and De-identification

Navigate the landscape of data anonymization and de-identification to protect individual privacy. Learn techniques within R to strip sensitive information from datasets while retaining their utility for analysis. Balancing data utility and privacy is a key consideration in the security playbook.

Securing R Code and Infrastructure

Code Security Best Practices

Uncover best practices for securing your R code against potential vulnerabilities. From input validation to code reviews, establish a robust code security framework that mitigates risks and ensures the reliability of your statistical analyses. Building secure code habits is fundamental in the defense against malicious exploits.

Access Controls and Authentication

Implement strong access controls and authentication mechanisms to fortify your R environment. Understand role-based access, multi-factor authentication, and other measures that control who can access what within your statistical computing ecosystem. Tightening the reins on access is a key strategy in preventing unauthorized entry.

Monitoring and Incident Response

Continuous Monitoring for Anomalies

Adopt a proactive stance by implementing continuous monitoring for anomalies. Explore tools and techniques within R to detect unusual patterns, unauthorized access, or potential security breaches. Real-time monitoring is a crucial component in maintaining a vigilant security posture.

Incident Response Planning

Understand the critical steps to take when a security breach occurs, including communication strategies, forensics, and remediation. Preparation and a well-defined response plan are pivotal in minimizing the impact of security incidents.

Emerging Trends and Future Considerations

Security in the Cloud Computing Era

Anticipate the evolving landscape of security considerations in the era of cloud computing. Explore how R programming interfaces with cloud environments and the unique security challenges and solutions associated with this paradigm shift. Staying ahead of cloud security trends is essential for modern statistical computing.

Integrating AI and Machine Learning for Security

Discover the role of artificial intelligence (AI) and machine learning (ML) in enhancing security measures. Explore how R interfaces with AI and ML technologies to predict, identify, and respond to security threats. Leveraging these technologies can provide a proactive and adaptive security framework.

Conclusion: Building a Strong Fortress for Statistical Computing

In conclusion, fortifying the castle of statistical computing involves a multifaceted approach that encompasses data protection, code security, access controls, and vigilant monitoring. This section equips you with the knowledge and tools needed to establish a strong fortress around your R programming environment.

As you navigate the intricacies of security measures in R programming, remember that the goal is not only to protect against current threats but also to anticipate and adapt to the evolving security landscape. By implementing robust security practices, you ensure that your statistical computing endeavors remain resilient, trustworthy, and secure in the face of an ever-changing digital landscape.

Data Privacy and Compliance: A Guide for R Users

In the era of heightened awareness surrounding data privacy and compliance, R users play a crucial role in ensuring the responsible handling of sensitive information. This section serves as a comprehensive guide, navigating the intricate landscape of data privacy regulations and compliance considerations within the context of R programming.

Navigating the Regulatory Terrain

Understanding Data Protection Regulations

Embark on a journey through key data protection regulations that shape the landscape of data privacy. From the General Data Protection Regulation (GDPR) to the California Consumer Privacy Act (CCPA), gain insights into the principles and requirements that influence how R users handle and process personal data.

Industry-Specific Compliance Considerations

Explore industry-specific regulations that impact data privacy in R programming. From the Health Insurance Portability and Accountability Act (HIPAA) in healthcare to the Financial Industry Regulatory Authority (FINRA) in finance, understand how compliance requirements vary across different sectors and tailor your R practices accordingly.

Best Practices for Data Privacy in R

Anonymization and Pseudonymization Techniques

Delve into anonymization and pseudonymization techniques within the R environment. Learn how to protect individual privacy by removing or encrypting personally identifiable information (PII) while still retaining the utility of the data for analysis. Balancing the need for privacy with analytical requirements is a central theme in data privacy best practices.

Data Impact Assessments

Integrate data impact assessments into your R workflow to systematically evaluate and address potential privacy risks. Understand how to identify, document, and mitigate privacy concerns associated with specific data processing activities. Data impact assessments contribute to a proactive and privacy-conscious approach in R programming.

Ethical Considerations in Data Science

The Role of Ethics in Data Science

Acknowledge the ethical dimensions of data science and the responsibilities that come with handling data. Explore ethical considerations related to consent, transparency, and fairness in the context of R programming. Upholding ethical standards is integral to fostering trust and accountability in data science practices.

Collaborating with Legal Experts

Recognize the importance of collaboration with legal experts to ensure compliance with data protection regulations. Learn how to establish effective communication channels with legal professionals, seek guidance on privacy matters, and incorporate legal reviews into your R programming workflow. Collaboration with legal experts enhances the robustness of your privacy measures.

Documentation and Transparency

Documenting Data Practices

Master the art of documenting data practices within R projects. Understand the components of comprehensive documentation, including metadata, data dictionaries, and data lineage. Well-documented data practices contribute to transparency and facilitate compliance audits, ensuring that R users can account for every step in the data processing lifecycle.

Transparent Reporting with R Markdown

Explore the use of R Markdown as a tool for transparent and auditable reporting. Learn how to integrate privacy-related information, compliance documentation, and data impact assessments directly into your R Markdown reports. Transparent reporting enhances accountability and provides stakeholders with a clear understanding of privacy considerations.

Future Trends and Continuous Learning

Emerging Trends in Data Privacy

Stay ahead of emerging trends in data privacy that may influence the landscape of R programming. Explore topics such as privacy-preserving techniques, federated learning, and evolving regulatory frameworks. Continuous learning is essential for R users to adapt to the evolving field of data privacy.

Building a Privacy-Centric Culture

Promote a privacy-centric culture within the R community and organizations at large. Emphasize the importance of privacy awareness, training, and ongoing education for R users. Cultivating a culture that values and prioritizes privacy contributes to a sustainable and ethical data science ecosystem.

Upholding Privacy in R Programming

In conclusion, navigating the terrain of data privacy and compliance is a shared responsibility among R users. This guide equips you with the knowledge and strategies needed to uphold privacy principles, comply with regulations, and foster an ethical and transparent data science environment within the realm of R programming.

As you navigate the complexities of data privacy, remember that privacy considerations are not static; they evolve with technological advancements, regulatory changes, and societal expectations. By embracing a privacy-centric mindset and integrating best practices into your R programming workflow, you contribute to a data landscape that respects individual privacy rights and maintains the trust of stakeholders.

R and Cybersecurity: Navigating Potential Threats

In the ever-expanding digital landscape, the intersection of R programming and cybersecurity is a critical frontier. This section serves as a guide for R users, navigating the intricate terrain of cybersecurity to fortify their statistical computing environments against potential threats. From code vulnerabilities to network security, understanding and mitigating cybersecurity risks is essential in maintaining the integrity of R programming endeavors.

Recognizing Cybersecurity Risks in R

Code Vulnerabilities and Best Practices

Explore the landscape of code vulnerabilities within R programming. Understand common pitfalls, such as injection attacks and insecure dependencies, and discover best practices for writing secure R code. Addressing code vulnerabilities is foundational to building a robust defense against potential cyber threats.

Network Security Considerations

Delve into network security considerations specific to R users. From securing data transmission to protecting against man-in-the-middle attacks, learn strategies to safeguard the communication channels used in R programming. Network security is a crucial aspect of maintaining the confidentiality and integrity of data flows.

Implementing Secure Coding Practices

Input Validation and Sanitization

Master the art of input validation and sanitization in R programming. Understand how to validate user inputs and sanitize data to prevent common security vulnerabilities, such as SQL injection and cross-site scripting. Implementing these practices contributes to building resilient R applications.

Secure Package Management

Navigate the realm of package management with a focus on security. Learn how to securely manage R packages, validate their integrity, and stay informed about potential security vulnerabilities. Proactive package management is essential in mitigating risks associated with third-party dependencies.

Access Controls and Authentication

Role-Based Access Controls

Implement role-based access controls within your R environment to regulate user permissions effectively. Learn how to assign roles, define access levels, and control user privileges based on their responsibilities. Access controls are pivotal in preventing unauthorized access to sensitive data and functionalities.

Multi-Factor Authentication (MFA)

Enhance authentication security by implementing multi-factor authentication (MFA). Explore the integration of MFA into your R programming environment to add an extra layer of identity verification. MFA mitigates the risk of unauthorized access, especially in scenarios where sensitive data is involved.

Monitoring for Anomalies and Incidents

Real-Time Monitoring for Security Anomalies

Establish a proactive security posture by implementing real-time monitoring for anomalies. Learn how to leverage tools and techniques within R to detect unusual patterns, potential security breaches, or unauthorized access. Real-time monitoring is a key component of identifying and responding to security incidents promptly.

Incident Response Planning in R

Develop an incident response plan tailored to the unique considerations of R programming. Understand the steps to take when a security incident occurs, including communication strategies, forensics, and remediation. Incident response planning ensures a swift and effective response to minimize the impact of security breaches.

Collaborating with Cybersecurity Experts

The Role of Cybersecurity Experts

Recognize the importance of collaboration with cybersecurity experts in fortifying your R programming environment. Learn how to engage with cybersecurity professionals, seek guidance on security matters, and incorporate cybersecurity reviews into your R workflow. Collaboration with experts enhances the overall security posture.

Security Awareness and Training

Promote security awareness and training among R users to cultivate a cybersecurity-conscious culture. Understand the significance of ongoing education, training sessions, and awareness campaigns to empower R users with the knowledge needed to identify and address potential security threats.

Future Trends and Continuous Vigilance

Emerging Trends in Cybersecurity

Stay abreast of emerging trends in cybersecurity that may impact the landscape of R programming. Explore topics such as threat intelligence, zero-trust architecture, and evolving attack vectors. Continuous vigilance is crucial in adapting security measures to the ever-changing cybersecurity landscape.

Building a Security-First Culture

Instill a security-first culture within the R community and organizations at large. Emphasize the importance of prioritizing security considerations in every aspect of R programming. Building a culture that values and integrates security measures contributes to a resilient and secure statistical computing ecosystem.

Safeguarding R Programming Against Cyber Threats

In conclusion, the intersection of R programming and cybersecurity demands a proactive and multifaceted approach to safeguard against potential threats. This section equips R users with the knowledge and strategies needed to fortify their statistical computing environments, ensuring the confidentiality, integrity, and availability of data.

As you navigate the complexities of cybersecurity risks in R, remember that cybersecurity is an ongoing journey. By integrating secure coding practices, implementing robust access controls, and collaborating with cybersecurity experts, you contribute to a security-conscious R community. Building a resilient defense against cyber threats is not only a technical imperative but also a shared responsibility among R users to protect the integrity of statistical computing endeavors.

Chapter 13: Community and Collaboration in R

Welcome to the vibrant realm of R, where a global community of data scientists, statisticians, and enthusiasts converge to share knowledge, collaborate on projects, and shape the future of data-driven decision-making. In this chapter, we embark on a journey to explore the power of community and collaboration in R, witnessing how this ecosystem fosters innovation, accelerates learning, and drives the advancement of data science.

The Essence of Community in R

The R community is a diverse and inclusive group of individuals united by their passion for data exploration, analysis, and visualization. This community extends far beyond geographical boundaries, encompassing individuals from all corners of the globe, connected through online forums, social media platforms, and professional organizations.

The R community is characterized by a culture of open sharing, where individuals freely contribute their knowledge, code, and expertise to the collective pool. This spirit of collaboration fuels innovation, as ideas are exchanged, refined, and translated into practical tools and methodologies.

Collaboration: Driving Innovation and Accelerating Learning

Collaboration within the R community manifests in diverse forms, ranging from informal online discussions to structured research projects. These collaborative efforts serve as a catalyst for innovation, enabling data scientists to tackle complex problems, develop novel approaches, and expand the boundaries of what's possible with data.

One of the most prominent examples of collaboration in R is the development and maintenance of R packages. A vast array of packages, each contributing a unique set of functionalities, has been created and refined through the collective efforts of the R community.

The R community also fosters collaboration through various events, conferences, and workshops. These gatherings provide opportunities for data scientists to connect, share ideas, and learn from each other's expertise, further strengthening the bonds of the community.

The Benefits of Community and Collaboration

Engaging with the R community offers numerous benefits for data scientists:

- Access to a Vast Knowledge Base: The collective knowledge of the R community serves as an invaluable resource, providing insights, solutions, and best practices for various data science tasks.

- Accelerated Learning and Problem-Solving: Collaboration with experienced data scientists fosters rapid learning and effective problem-solving, enabling individuals to tackle challenges more efficiently.

- Inspiration and Innovation: The exchange of ideas and diverse perspectives stimulates creativity and innovation, leading to the development of new approaches and tools.

- Professional Networking and Growth: The R community provides a platform for professional networking, opening doors to collaboration opportunities and career advancement.

The R community is an integral part of the data science landscape, providing a supportive and collaborative environment where individuals can learn, innovate, and contribute to the advancement of data-driven solutions. By actively engaging with the community, data scientists can leverage the collective expertise and diverse perspectives to tackle complex challenges, extract meaningful insights from data, and shape the future of data science.

Building Bridges:

Networking in the R Community

The R community, as a vibrant ecosystem of data scientists, statisticians, and enthusiasts, provides a plethora of opportunities to connect, collaborate, and expand your professional network. By actively engaging with the community, you can gain valuable insights, foster meaningful partnerships, and enhance your career prospects. Let's explore some effective strategies to build bridges within the R community:

Embrace Online Platforms:

The R community thrives in the digital realm, with various online platforms serving as hubs for interaction and knowledge sharing. Engage in online forums and discussion groups, such as RStudio Community, Stack Overflow, and Reddit's r/RStudio and r/Rlanguage, to connect with fellow R users, ask questions, and contribute your expertise.

Attend R-Conferences and Events:

Regularly attend R conferences and events, such as useR!, RConf, and SatRday, to network with peers, learn from industry experts, and stay updated on the latest developments in the R ecosystem. These events provide a dynamic environment for exchanging ideas, forging collaborations, and expanding your professional circle.

Contribute to Open-Source Projects:

Get involved in open-source R projects to showcase your skills, gain hands-on experience, and contribute to the community's growth. Participating in open-source projects allows you to collaborate with experienced developers, learn from their expertise, and build a strong reputation within the community.

Engage with Local R Groups:

Join local R user groups or meetups to connect with R enthusiasts in your area. These local gatherings provide opportunities for face-to-face interaction, hands-on workshops, and mentorship from experienced R practitioners.

Share Your Knowledge and Expertise:

Become a knowledge sharer by creating blog posts, tutorials, and presentations on R-related topics. Sharing your expertise not only establishes you as a thought leader but also contributes to the collective learning of the community.

Leverage Social Media Platforms:

Connect with R experts and enthusiasts on social media platforms like Twitter and LinkedIn. Engage in discussions, share relevant content, and actively participate in online communities to expand your network and stay informed about industry trends.

Contribute to R Packages:

If you have programming skills, consider contributing to the development and maintenance of R packages. This involvement not only enhances your coding proficiency but also demonstrates your commitment to the community's growth.

Seek Mentorship and Guidance:

Seek mentorship from experienced R practitioners to gain valuable insights, career advice, and guidance as you navigate your professional journey. Mentorship can provide invaluable support and accelerate your personal and professional growth.

By embracing these networking strategies, you can effectively build bridges within the R community, fostering meaningful connections, expanding your professional network, and establishing yourself as a valuable contributor to the data science landscape.

Collaborative Coding: GitHub and Version Control

In the dynamic realm of data science, collaboration is key to tackling complex problems, achieving innovative solutions, and accelerating the pace of discovery. GitHub, a cloud-based hosting service for version control, has emerged as an indispensable tool for data scientists to collaborate effectively and manage their code repositories.

Embracing Version Control: A Foundation for Collaborative Coding

Version control is a fundamental practice in software development, enabling developers to track changes to their code, revert to previous versions, and maintain a comprehensive history of project development. This practice is crucial for collaborative coding, as it provides a centralized repository where multiple developers can work on the same codebase without conflicts or inconsistencies.

GitHub, with its user-friendly interface and comprehensive features, has become the de-facto standard for version control in the data science community. It provides a secure platform for storing code repositories, tracking changes, and managing access control, enabling data scientists to collaborate seamlessly.

The Collaborative Coding Workflow with GitHub

The collaborative coding workflow with GitHub typically involves the following steps:

1. Creating a Repository: Establish a new repository on GitHub to store the project code.

2. Forking and Cloning the Repository: Fork the repository to create a personal copy. This copy allows you to make changes without affecting the original repository. Clone the forked repository to your local machine to work on the code locally.

3. Making Changes and Committing: Modify the code as needed, adding new features, fixing bugs, or implementing new algorithms. Commit your changes with descriptive messages, providing a clear record of the modifications made.

4. Pushing Changes to GitHub: Push your committed changes to your forked repository on GitHub. This updates the remote repository with your local changes.

5. Creating a Pull Request: Create a pull request to propose your changes to the original repository. This request initiates a review process where the repository owner or collaborators can review and discuss your modifications before merging them into the main codebase.

6. Merging Changes: Once the pull request is approved, merge your changes into the original repository. This integrates your contributions into the main codebase, making them available to all collaborators.

GitHub Features for Collaborative Coding

GitHub offers a suite of features that facilitate effective collaboration among data scientists:

- Issue Tracking: Create and manage issues to track bugs, feature requests, and tasks, ensuring that everyone is aligned on project priorities and progress.

- Code Review and Discussion: Utilize the code review feature to provide feedback on others' code, ensuring that contributions adhere to coding standards and best practices.

- Project Management: Utilize GitHub Projects to organize tasks, assign responsibilities, and track progress, ensuring that the project remains on track and deliverables are met.

Benefits of Collaborative Coding with GitHub

Collaborative coding with GitHub offers several benefits:

- Improved Code Quality: Peer review and collaboration lead to higher quality code, identifying and fixing errors early in the development process.

- Efficient Project Management: Clear task assignment, issue tracking, and progress monitoring foster efficient project management and collaboration.

- Knowledge Sharing and Learning: Collaboration encourages knowledge exchange and peer learning, enabling data scientists to learn from each other's expertise.

- Reproducible Research: Version control provides a comprehensive history of code changes, ensuring reproducibility of research findings and models.

GitHub has revolutionized the way data scientists collaborate, providing a centralized platform for code management, version control, and seamless teamwork. By embracing collaborative coding practices and utilizing GitHub's powerful features, data scientists can accelerate their research, enhance code quality, and achieve greater success in their data-driven endeavors. As the field of data science continues to evolve, collaborative coding will remain an essential practice, enabling data scientists to tackle complex problems and shape the future of data-driven innovation.

Contribute and Thrive: Becoming an Active Member of the R Community

The R community is a thriving ecosystem of data scientists, statisticians, and enthusiasts, united by their passion for data exploration, analysis, and visualization. This vibrant community welcomes individuals from diverse backgrounds and skill levels, offering opportunities to learn, collaborate, and contribute to the advancement of data science.

The Essence of Contribution in the R Community

Contribution is the lifeblood of the R community. It's through the collective efforts of individuals sharing their knowledge, expertise, and code that the community thrives, expands, and drives innovation. Every contribution, no matter how small, has the potential to make a significant impact on the community and shape the future of data science.

Ways to Contribute to the R Community

The R community offers a multitude of avenues for individuals to contribute and make a meaningful impact:

1. Share Your Knowledge: Write blog posts, tutorials, and documentation to share your expertise with others. This act of knowledge sharing not only helps others learn but also establishes you as a thought leader in the community.

2. Contribute to Open-Source Projects: Get involved in open-source R projects by contributing code, fixing bugs, and improving existing functionalities. This involvement not only enhances your coding skills but also demonstrates your commitment to the community's growth.

3. Engage in Online Discussions: Actively participate in online forums, discussion groups, and social media communities to share your insights, answer questions, and provide guidance to others. Your participation helps foster a supportive and collaborative environment for learning and growth.

4. Give Presentations and Workshops: Share your expertise by giving presentations and workshops at local R user groups, conferences, and online events. This allows you to directly connect with others and inspire them to explore new data science techniques.

5. Mentor and Guide Others: Offer mentorship and guidance to aspiring data scientists and beginners. Share your experiences, provide constructive feedback, and help them navigate their learning journey.

6. Contribute to R Documentation: Improve the quality and comprehensiveness of R documentation by submitting pull requests, correcting errors, and suggesting enhancements. This contribution directly benefits the community's ability to learn and utilize R effectively.

7. Organize Events and Meetups: Take the initiative to organize local R user groups, meetups, and workshops

to bring together data scientists in your area. These events foster collaboration, networking, and knowledge exchange.

Benefits of Active Contribution

Contributing to the R community offers numerous benefits for individuals:

- Enhanced Learning and Skill Development: By contributing, you actively engage with the latest advancements in data science and expand your knowledge base.

- Recognition and Reputation: Your contributions are recognized and valued by the community, establishing you as an expert and thought leader.

- Professional Networking and Growth: Active participation expands your professional network, leading to potential collaborations and career opportunities.

- Personal Fulfillment and Satisfaction: Contributing to a shared goal brings a sense of fulfillment and satisfaction, knowing that your efforts are making a positive impact.

Conclusion

The R community is a welcoming and supportive environment where individuals of all skill levels can contribute, learn, and grow. By actively engaging with the community, sharing your knowledge, and contributing your expertise, you can make a meaningful impact on the advancement of data science and reap personal and professional rewards. As you embark on your journey within the R community, remember that every contribution, no matter how small, has the potential to make a significant difference. Embrace the spirit of collaboration, share your passion for data, and thrive as an active member of this vibrant community.

Chapter 14: R Ecosystem Explorations: Harnessing the Power of R Packages

An Introduction to the R Package Universe

In the dynamic realm of data science, R packages have emerged as indispensable tools, empowering data scientists to tackle complex problems with efficiency and creativity. These specialized packages provide a vast array of functionalities, ranging from data manipulation and analysis to machine learning and statistical modeling.

The R package ecosystem is expansive and ever-evolving, with thousands of packages available to cater to diverse data science needs. From specialized packages for specific domains to general-purpose tools for data wrangling and visualization, the R package universe offers a treasure trove of resources for data scientists to explore and utilize.

Navigating the R Package Landscape

Navigating the vast R package landscape can be challenging, given the sheer number of available packages and the varying levels of maturity and documentation. To effectively discover and utilize the right packages for your tasks, consider the following strategies:

- Identify Your Needs: Clearly define the data analysis, visualization, or modeling task you aim to accomplish. This will help you narrow down your search and focus on packages relevant to your specific needs.

- Seek Guidance and Recommendations: Consult online resources, such as CRAN (Comprehensive R Archive Network), RStudio's package manager, and online forums, to gather recommendations and insights from experienced data scientists.

- Read Documentation and Examples: Before installing a package, thoroughly review its documentation, including its functions, usage examples, and vignettes. This will provide insights into the package's capabilities, limitations, and suitability for your task.

- Explore Package Repositories: Utilize online repositories like CRAN and GitHub to browse packages, filter based on keywords or categories, and gain an overview of their functionalities and popularity.

Unlocking the Power of R Packages

Once you've identified the appropriate packages for your task, effectively integrating them into your workflow requires a structured approach:

- Installation and Setup: Install the packages using the appropriate package manager, ensuring compatibility with your R version and operating system.

- Package Loading: Load the packages into your R session using the library() function, making their functions and data structures accessible within your environment.

- Exploring Package Contents: Familiarize yourself with the package's contents using tools like help() and ? to access documentation and examples.

- Applying Package Functionalities: Utilize the package's functions and data structures within your code to perform data manipulation, analysis, visualization, or modeling tasks.

- Keeping Packages Updated: Regularly check for updates to the packages you use, ensuring you have the latest versions with bug fixes and performance improvements.

The Impact of R Packages on Data Science

R packages have revolutionized the way data science is conducted, bringing about several transformative impacts:

- Enhanced Efficiency and Productivity: Packages provide specialized tools for various data science tasks, streamlining workflows and reducing development time.

- Reproducibility and Transparency: Packages promote reproducible research by providing consistent and well-documented code that can be shared and reused.

- Expanding Data Science Capabilities: Packages continually expand the capabilities of R, introducing new algorithms, techniques, and visualizations.

- Community Collaboration and Innovation: Packages foster collaboration and knowledge sharing within the R community, driving innovation and accelerating advancements.

The R package ecosystem is a vibrant and ever-evolving landscape, offering data scientists a wealth of specialized tools to tackle complex problems with efficiency and creativity. By effectively navigating this vast repository of packages, data scientists can harness the power of R to extract meaningful insights from data, build robust predictive models, and shape the future of data-driven decision-making. As you venture into the world of R packages, remember that continuous learning, exploration, and engagement with the community will empower you to become a proficient and innovative data scientist, capable of making significant contributions to the ever-expanding field of data science.

R Package Ecosystem: Exploring the Treasure Trove of Data Science Tools

Navigating the Sea of R Packages

The R package ecosystem is a vast and ever-evolving landscape, offering data scientists a treasure trove of specialized tools to tackle complex problems with efficiency and creativity. From data manipulation and visualization to machine learning and statistical modeling, R packages cater to diverse data science needs.

To effectively navigate this vast repository, consider the following strategies:

- Identify Your Needs: Clearly define the data analysis, visualization, or modeling task you aim to accomplish. This will help you narrow down your search and focus on packages relevant to your specific needs.

- Seek Guidance and Recommendations: Consult online resources, such as CRAN (Comprehensive R Archive Network), RStudio's package manager, and online forums, to gather recommendations and insights from experienced data scientists.

- Read Documentation and Examples: Before installing a package, thoroughly review its documentation, including its functions, usage examples, and vignettes. This will provide insights into the package's capabilities, limitations, and suitability for your task.

- Explore Package Repositories: Utilize online repositories like CRAN and GitHub to browse packages, filter based on keywords or categories, and gain an overview of their functionalities and popularity.

Unearthing Hidden Gems: Exploring Lesser-Known R Packages

Venture beyond the familiar and explore the lesser-known corners of the R package repository to uncover hidden gems, offering unique capabilities and functionalities. These niche packages can address specific data science challenges, enhance data visualization techniques, or introduce novel statistical modeling approaches.

Here are a few examples of hidden gems worth exploring:

- data.table: An incredibly fast and efficient data manipulation package, offering superior performance over base R data frames and providing a wide range of flexible data management tools.

- ggplot2: A powerful and versatile data visualization package, known for its aesthetic and customizable plots, enabling data scientists to create informative and visually appealing visualizations.

- caret: A comprehensive toolkit for training, tuning, and evaluating machine learning models, providing a streamlined process for developing and optimizing predictive models.

- tidyverse: A collection of packages that share a consistent design philosophy, grammar, and data structures, promoting a unified and cohesive data science workflow.

- shiny: An innovative package for creating interactive web applications directly from R, enabling data scientists to share their insights and analyses with a wider audience in a dynamic and engaging manner.

Crafting Your Signature: Building and Sharing R Packages

The world of R packages is not just about consuming and utilizing existing tools; it also presents an exciting opportunity to create and share your own signature packages. By developing your own packages, you can contribute to the growing ecosystem of data science tools, address specific challenges in your domain, and showcase your expertise and innovation.

To build an R package, follow these steps:

1. Concept Development: Clearly define the purpose and functionality of your package. Identify the problems it solves, the target audience, and the unique contributions it makes to the data science landscape.

2. Code Design and Implementation: Write clean, well-documented code that adheres to R programming best practices. Utilize modularity, testing, and documentation to ensure the package's functionality, maintainability, and usability.

3. Package Structure and Organization: Structure your package following R package guidelines, including the

creation of a DESCRIPTION file, a NAMESPACE file, and appropriate directory structure.

4. Package Testing and Validation: Rigorously test your package using various testing frameworks, ensuring it functions as intended and handles various data types and scenarios.

5. Documentation and User Experience: Provide comprehensive documentation, including function descriptions, usage examples, and vignettes, to guide users in effectively utilizing your package.

Once your package is ready to share, follow these steps to make it accessible to the wider R community:

1. Create a GitHub Repository: Establish a GitHub repository to store your package code, documentation, and version control history.

2. Package Submission to CRAN: Submit your package to CRAN, the official repository of R packages, for review and consideration for inclusion.

3. Package Publication and Dissemination: Once accepted, your package will be available for installation through CRAN and other package repositories. Promote your

package through online communities, forums, and publications.

Benefits of Sharing Your R Package

Sharing your R package offers several benefits:

- Contribution to the Data Science Community: Your package expands the data science toolkit, providing valuable tools for others to address their data-driven challenges.

- Recognition and Reputation: Showcase your expertise and innovation, gaining recognition within the data science community.

- Feedback and Collaboration: Seek and receive feedback from users, leading to improvements and new features.

The potential impact of sharing your R package extends far beyond personal recognition and community contributions. By making your tools available to a broader audience, you empower organizations and researchers to tackle real-world problems, drive data-driven decision-making, and make a tangible difference in various domains.

Consider the following scenarios:

- A healthcare organization implements your machine learning package to develop predictive models for disease diagnosis and treatment optimization, improving patient care and outcomes.

- A financial institution utilizes your statistical modeling package to assess risk profiles and make informed investment decisions, enhancing financial stability and market performance.

- A research team employs your data visualization package to create compelling presentations and interactive dashboards, effectively communicating their findings to stakeholders and policymakers.

- A government agency leverages your data manipulation package to streamline data management and analysis, enabling data-driven policy formulation and resource allocation.

These examples illustrate the transformative power of sharing your R package. By contributing your expertise and innovation to the open-source community, you have the potential to make a significant impact on various industries, research endeavors, and societal challenges.

Conclusion: Embracing the Collaborative Spirit

The R package ecosystem thrives on collaboration, knowledge sharing, and the collective efforts of data scientists worldwide. By actively contributing to this ecosystem, you not only expand your own skillset and expertise but also contribute to the advancement of data science as a whole.

Embrace the collaborative spirit of the R community, share your knowledge and expertise, and unleash the potential of your R packages to make a meaningful impact on the world.

Chapter 15: Future Horizons: Trends and Innovations in R Programming

As the landscape of data science and statistical computing continues to evolve, Chapter 15 embarks on a journey into the future horizons of R programming. This chapter serves as a compass, guiding R enthusiasts through the emerging trends, innovative methodologies, and transformative technologies that are reshaping the way we approach statistical analysis and data-driven decision-making.

In this exploration of future horizons, we cast our gaze beyond the current state of R programming, delving into the frontiers of innovation that promise to redefine the capabilities and possibilities of this versatile language. From cutting-edge technologies to paradigm-shifting methodologies, this chapter offers a glimpse into the exciting developments that will shape the future of R programming.

As we navigate through the upcoming trends and innovations, anticipate insightful discussions on the integration of R with emerging technologies such as artificial intelligence and machine learning, the evolution of data visualization techniques, and the impact of R in interdisciplinary collaborations. The future of R programming is not merely about incremental improvements but a visionary journey into uncharted territories.

Whether you are a seasoned R user or just beginning your exploration, Chapter 15 invites you to peer into the crystal ball of R programming, where the boundaries of possibility are continually expanding. Join us in this forward-looking exploration, where trends transform into traditions and innovations become integral parts of the R programming tapestry. The future awaits, and the possibilities are as boundless as the imagination of the R community.

Beyond the Horizon:

Emerging Technologies in Data Science

In the dynamic landscape of data science, the horizon is ever-expanding, offering glimpses into the transformative potential of emerging technologies that will shape the future of R programming. This section, "Beyond the Horizon: Emerging Technologies in Data Science," serves as a portal into the frontiers where innovation converges with R, opening new avenues for exploration and discovery.

Integration of R with Artificial Intelligence (AI)

Machine Learning Integration

Embark on a journey where R seamlessly integrates with the realm of artificial intelligence. Explore how machine learning algorithms, ranging from classical models to deep learning architectures, are being woven into the fabric of R programming. The synergy between R and AI propels data science into uncharted territories, enabling the creation of intelligent and adaptive models.

Automated Machine Learning (AutoML)

Peer into the realm of automated machine learning (AutoML) within the context of R programming. Discover how AutoML frameworks empower users to automate the end-to-end process of building, tuning, and deploying machine learning models. The democratization of machine learning through AutoML redefines accessibility, making advanced modeling approaches more attainable for a broader audience.

Advancements in Big Data Processing

Scalability and Parallel Computing

Explore the advancements in big data processing within the R ecosystem. Delve into techniques that enhance the scalability of R for processing large datasets, including parallel computing and distributed computing frameworks. As the volume of data continues to grow, these innovations ensure that R remains a robust tool for analyzing and extracting insights from massive datasets.

Integration with Spark and Distributed Computing

Witness the integration of R with Apache Spark and other distributed computing platforms. Uncover how these integrations leverage the power of distributed computing to handle big data challenges efficiently. The marriage of R and distributed computing technologies accelerates data processing and analytics on a scale previously unattainable.

Evolution of Data Visualization Techniques

Interactive and Dynamic Visualizations

Step into the future of data visualization as R evolves to deliver interactive and dynamic visualizations. Explore the integration of interactive elements, allowing users to engage with visualizations dynamically. From responsive dashboards to real-time updates, these innovations enhance the communicative power of R-generated visual narratives.

3D and Augmented Reality Visualizations

Peer into the world of three-dimensional (3D) and augmented reality (AR) visualizations facilitated by R. Witness how these immersive technologies transform the presentation of complex data into interactive and engaging experiences. The evolution of visualizations in R extends beyond traditional boundaries, providing new perspectives for exploration.

Interdisciplinary Collaborations and R

Fusion with Domain-Specific Tools

Experience the fusion of R with domain-specific tools and technologies. Explore how R is becoming an integral part of interdisciplinary collaborations, seamlessly integrating with tools used in biology, finance, healthcare, and other domains. This convergence empowers experts from diverse fields to leverage R's analytical prowess in their specialized domains.

R in Cross-Disciplinary Research

Uncover the role of R in cross-disciplinary research, where data scientists collaborate with experts from various fields. Learn how R serves as a common language for interdisciplinary teams, facilitating the integration of statistical analysis and data-driven insights into broader research endeavors. The synergy between R and diverse disciplines fosters innovation and accelerates discovery.

Closing Thoughts: Embracing the Future

As we venture beyond the horizon of current possibilities, the integration of emerging technologies into R programming unfolds a landscape of limitless potential. This section serves as a glimpse into the exciting future where R evolves in tandem with technological advancements, shaping the way we approach data science, analysis, and collaboration.

The journey continues as R enthusiasts embrace these emerging technologies, pushing the boundaries of what's conceivable and laying the foundation for the next era of data-driven exploration. The fusion of R with artificial intelligence, advancements in big data processing, evolution in data visualization, and interdisciplinary collaborations marks a paradigm shift, heralding a future where the possibilities are as vast as the collective imagination of the R community.

The Next Frontier: Predictions for the Future of R Programming

As we stand at the precipice of the future, envisioning the next frontier of R programming becomes a thrilling endeavor. This section, "The Next Frontier: Predictions for the Future of R Programming," invites you to peer into the crystal ball of technological evolution and anticipate the trajectories that will shape the destiny of R. From innovative features to transformative methodologies, these predictions serve as a compass for navigating the uncharted territories that lie ahead.

Integration with Edge Computing

Anticipate the integration of R programming with edge computing technologies. As the demand for real-time analytics and decentralized processing grows, R is poised to extend its reach to the edge of networks, enabling data scientists to deploy models and perform analyses closer to the data source. This integration holds the promise of enhanced efficiency and responsiveness in data science workflows.

Evolution of Explainable AI in R

Foresee the evolution of explainable artificial intelligence (AI) within the R ecosystem. Recognizing the increasing importance of transparent and interpretable machine learning models, R is likely to witness advancements in tools and methodologies that demystify complex algorithms. Explainable AI in R ensures that model outcomes are not only accurate but also comprehensible to diverse stakeholders.

Proliferation of R in Education and Research

Envision the proliferation of R programming in educational institutions and research endeavors. As R continues to gain prominence for its accessibility and versatility, it is expected to become a cornerstone in educational curricula and a go-to tool for researchers across disciplines. This widespread adoption will contribute to a global community of R users with diverse skill sets and applications.

Enhanced Support for Collaboration and Version Control

Envisage enhanced support for collaboration and version control within the R environment. As interdisciplinary collaborations become more prevalent, R is likely to embrace tools and workflows that facilitate seamless collaboration among data scientists, statisticians, and domain experts. The integration of robust version control mechanisms will ensure reproducibility and transparency in collaborative projects.

Charting Your Course: Continuous Learning in the Dynamic World of R

In the dynamic world of R programming, the journey doesn't end; it transforms into a continuous odyssey of learning and growth. This section, "Charting Your Course: Continuous Learning in the Dynamic World of R," serves as a compass for R enthusiasts navigating the ever-evolving landscape. Whether you are a seasoned practitioner or a novice explorer, embracing continuous learning is essential for staying relevant and thriving in the vibrant R community.

Embracing Lifelong Learning

Acknowledge the ethos of lifelong learning as a fundamental principle in the R community. Embrace a mindset that values curiosity and a commitment to staying abreast of evolving technologies, methodologies, and best practices. Lifelong learning is not just a practice; it's a cultural cornerstone that fuels innovation and excellence in R programming.

Leveraging Online Resources and Communities

Harness the power of online resources and vibrant communities within the R ecosystem. Explore a wealth of tutorials, forums, and documentation that cater to learners of all levels. Engage with online communities to seek advice, share insights, and collaborate with fellow R enthusiasts. The collective wisdom of the community is an invaluable asset in your learning journey.

Exploring Specialized Training and Certification

Consider exploring specialized training programs and certifications to deepen your expertise in specific R domains. From advanced statistical modeling to data visualization and machine learning, specialized training equips you with targeted skills and knowledge. Certifications serve as tangible milestones, validating your proficiency and enhancing your credibility in the R community and beyond.

Contributing to Open Source Projects

Participate in the collaborative spirit of open source by contributing to R packages and projects. Engaging with the open source community not only allows you to give back but also provides hands-on experience in real-world R development. Contributing to open source projects is a symbiotic relationship, fostering a culture of shared knowledge and innovation.

Networking and Collaboration

Recognize the value of networking and collaboration in the expansive world of R programming. Attend conferences, workshops, and meetups to connect with like-minded individuals, experts, and thought leaders. Building a professional network not only opens doors to opportunities but also cultivates a supportive ecosystem for continuous learning and career advancement.

A Lifelong Journey in R Programming

In conclusion, the dynamic world of R programming beckons you on a lifelong journey of exploration, discovery, and continuous learning. As you chart your course in this vibrant landscape, remember that the true essence of R programming lies not just in the code you write but in the community you engage with and the knowledge you share.

Embrace the spirit of curiosity, stay curious, and let the evolving horizons of R programming be your inspiration. The journey is yours to navigate, and as you embark on this lifelong odyssey, may each line of code be a step forward, each challenge a learning opportunity, and each collaboration a chapter in your ever-expanding story of mastery in R programming.

Conclusion

Navigating the R Programming Odyssey

As we draw the final curtain on this exploration into the vast realm of R programming, we reflect on the journey that has unfolded throughout the chapters of this book. From the foundational principles to the advanced frontiers, each page has been a stepping stone in the odyssey of mastering R programming. As we conclude, let's pause to distill the essence of our shared venture.

A Tapestry of Knowledge and Skills

The chapters within this book have woven a tapestry of knowledge and skills, embracing novices and seasoned practitioners alike. Whether you embarked on this journey with a blank canvas or a palette of experiences, the intention was to provide insights, practical wisdom, and a roadmap for your growth as an R programmer.

Building a Solid Foundation

At the outset, we laid the groundwork with the fundamentals— the syntax, data structures, and programming paradigms that form the bedrock of R programming. These foundational elements serve as the compass, guiding you through the intricate pathways of data manipulation, statistical analysis, and visualization.

Mastery of Data Science Tools

The chapters unfolded to reveal the expansive toolbox that R offers to data scientists. From tidyverse packages for data wrangling to advanced statistical modeling techniques, R has proven to be a versatile companion in the pursuit of actionable insights from data. The integration of R Markdown and Shiny showcased the narrative and interactive capabilities that elevate your reports and dashboards.

Ethical Considerations and Responsible Practices

Acknowledging the ethical dimensions of data science, we delved into the importance of responsible practices. From the ethical compass guiding your data science endeavors to considerations of data privacy and compliance, we emphasized the significance of upholding ethical standards in every facet of your R programming journey.

Security and Future Horizons

Fortifying your statistical castle against potential threats, we navigated through the realms of security in statistical computing. As we gazed into the crystal ball of the future, we explored emerging technologies, predictions for the future of R programming, and the continuous learning imperative to stay ahead in the dynamic landscape of data science.

A Lifelong Odyssey

The journey of mastering R programming is not a destination but a lifelong odyssey. It is a commitment to continuous learning, curiosity-driven exploration, and the cultivation of a community spirit. As the R programming ecosystem evolves, so too does the journey, offering new challenges, opportunities, and horizons to explore.

Your Story in R Programming

Ultimately, the story of mastering R programming is not just about the code you write or the analyses you conduct. It's about the narratives you craft with your data, the impact you make with your insights, and the collaborations that enrich your journey. Each R user contributes a unique chapter to the collective narrative of the R community.

As you turn the final page of this book, consider it not an endpoint but a waypoint in your R programming expedition. The odyssey continues, and the possibilities are as boundless as your curiosity and dedication. May your code be elegant, your analyses insightful, and your journey in R programming an ever-inspiring exploration into the art and science of data. Happy coding!